What People are Saying about

GETTING THRU TO YOUR SOUL
AND SPIRITUAL KINESIOLOGY

"The authors write with a clarity and compassion that speaks to our souls."
						–David Richo
				author of *Unexpected Miracles: The Gift of Synchronicity*

"*Getting Thru to Your Soul* is a must if you seek the deeper meaning in life. This wonderful book goes beyond describing why you should connect with your soul and gives you the tools to reach your goal. The processes are simple, profound and permanent! They have even helped me see that my upcoming surgery is a gift that will bring more love and understanding into my life. Thanks to the information and techniques in this book, I'm living more of my life from a place of peace and tranquility."
						–Katherine Zimmerman
						author of *Breakthrough: EFT*

"Never before have I seen the inner self shown so strongly."
					–Lillian McIntryre, Somatic Practitioner

"I have dealt with this very difficult relationship with my father before, but in one Spiritual Kinesiology session, all the emotional charge was gone. Now I can actually appreciate the good (and insecure) man that my father was, and, to my surprise, admire some very wonderful qualities he had. The life-long hurt and resentment are gone, and that feels so good!"
					–Mary Ann Michels, Hypno-Energy Therapist

"I love this book because it gives such concrete information that shows you how to unify with your soul. It helped me work through an issue of getting help and support for my needs in the future. Books rarely deal with the all-important subject of how to live a soul-based life – and this one does so clearly and practically. I thoroughly recommend it!" –Sharon Shiflett
Teacher

"You can put the information and processes to use immediately. Using the Integration Process, I experienced an amazing integration of my male and female energies. And it was much easier to do than I had imagined." –Sarah Paulhamus
Custodian, student

"I've never experienced so much light coming from a book before. My heart started glowing as I read it. And the Spiritual Kinesiology helped the degenerating vision in my eye return to a normal state. Spiritual Kinesiology reveals the exact route of any problem's descent from the spiritual source down to the physical, providing a clear channel through which the soul can send the specific energy required to transform the situation. This process and the entire book is fabulous!" –Mary Jaworski
Business Administrator

"The processes change the resonating frequency of any issue to conform to your natural frequency. It's like fine-tuning a radio, reducing the static from other outside interference to pure clarity of inner peace. A profound process." –Terry Burke
Pharmacist, Hypnotherapist, Reiki Master

"I have used the processes in this book for such usual things as headaches, fatigue, and those aches and pains we all get. But I didn't realize how much I had changed until last week, when I was stuck on the ground in a very uncomfortable airplane, and what should have been a five-hour trip took eleven hours – and what's more, my luggage never came back. Remarkably, I never once got impatient, frustrated, or angry. I simply accepted the situation without fighting it, and enjoyed the novel I brought with me as well as pleasant conversations with my fellow passengers. This was very unlike my typical 'volcanic' reaction – and it felt great!"   –Jean Hofve

Animal Rights Advocate

"I found this very readable book to be a great bridge between traditional techniques and new methods. The processes have immediate results and enhance the spiritual activations for living a more soulful life."   –Dana I. McKnight

Social Worker, Educator, Reiki Master

"The shame I had held for many years over the abuse from my mother was totally released with these techniques. I am amazed how quickly the Heart Focus process transformed a state that had burdened me for many years. The weight is gone. I now feel light and joyful, and I understand my own sense of power for the first time."   –Juanita Tayabas

Technical Writer, Reiki Master

"Bringing in my soul's energy has allowed instantaneous healing of emotionally charged situations, such as a relationship I had with a person who was difficult to work with. This book offers powerful, easy-to-use processes designed to anchor your soul's wisdom in all aspects of your life."   –Steve Chroniak

Book Store Events Coordinator, Yoga and Meditation Teacher

"The wonderful processes in this book helped me clear blockages and disconnections in myself and my relationship with my twenty-two year old son. Now our boundaries and communication are much better."   –Richard Fry

Pharmacist, Hypnotherapist, Reiki Master

Book and Cover Design
By Jane Mountrose

GETTING THRU
TO YOUR SOUL

Phillip Mountrose and Jane Mountrose

Holistic Communications
Sacramento, California

Published by: Holistic Communications
                 P.O. Box 279
                 Arroyo Grande, CA 93421-0279 USA
                 E-mail: awake@gettingthru.org

ISBN: 0-9653787-0-5
Library of Congress Catalog Card Number: 00-190043

Publisher's Cataloging-in-Publication
   (*Provided by Quality Books Inc.*)

Mountrose, Phillip.
Getting thru to your soul / Phillip Mountrose
and Jane Mountrose – 1ˢᵗ ed..
p. cm – (Getting thru)
Includes biographical references and index.
LCCN: 00-190043
ISBN 0-9653787-0-5
1. Soul. 2 Self-actualization (Psychology).
I. Mountrose, Jane. II. Title.

BF1045.S44M68 2000   158.1
                      QBI00-261

Acknowledgments

This book is about connecting with your soul and living a soul-based life. We have been fortunate to meet many wonderful and talented people who have contributed to our understanding. They have helped us in innumerable ways as we have moved forward on our own journeys of self-discovery, and in the development of the techniques we use in our work of helping others.

We want to thank Barry Snyder and Karen Anderson for leading us on the path that has produced the Getting Thru Techniques. We also want to thank Carl Carpenter for sharing his pioneering work with Hypno-Kinesiology, which has transformed the lives of many people.

In addition, we thank Briana Finley, Dana McKnight, Steven Chroniak, Sharon Shiflett, and Katherine Zimmerman for their insightful input in the writing of this book. Also, we would like to add our appreciation to all of the people who, through classes and personal consultations, have provided examples for this book, and helped us to refine our use of the techniques. They have generously given us encouragement and invaluable support.

Publisher's Disclaimer

Spiritual Kinesiology (SK) and the Getting Thru Techniques (GTT) have helped many people to make positive changes in their lives, but there is no guarantee they will work for you. We do not recommend substituting these techniques for the professional services of a doctor, psychologist or psychiatrist. Please consult your medical health professionals regarding their use.

SK and GTT are self-help and self-healing techniques, and you are in control of their use. As such, you have sole responsibility when you use them. If you do not wish to be bound by this disclaimer, you may return this book with proof of purchase to the publisher for a full refund.

Table of Contents

xii

Table of Figures

The Soul Beckons

*To live happily
is an inward power of the soul.*

–MARCUS AURELIUS

With the growing emergence of spiritual awareness, this is an exciting time to be alive. Many people are responding to the calls of their souls and experiencing profound spiritual awakenings. In our roles as spiritual teachers and counselors, "What is my soul's purpose?" is the question we are asked most frequently. Soul purpose is also a subject that each person has to examine and understand individually for the answer to have true meaning. Helping you to understand and live your divine purpose is the focus of *Getting Thru to Your Soul*.

Our interest in soul awareness and spirituality has taken us on a 25-year journey of self-discovery, most recently as Holistic Hypnotherapists, Neurolinguistic Programming (NLP) Practitioners, Reiki Masters, Clairvoyant Counselors, and Ministers of Holistic Healing. Together, we operate a school for personal and spiritual development, the Awakenings Institute, and assist students and clients on their spiritual paths both locally and by phone throughout the United States. Phillip also has over 20 years of experience in education, including work with emotionally disturbed teenage boys. He has shared some of this experience in his two books *Getting Thru to Kids: The 5 Steps to Problem Solving with Children Ages 6 to 18* and *Tips and Tools for Getting Thru to Kids.*

In our roles as teachers and counselors, we can see that the light and wisdom of the soul is available to every one of us. The truth of its existence as our most powerful healer and divine guide transcends our age group, nationality, education, income level, and religious orientation. The soul honors the uniqueness of each individual while it creates a common bond that unites us all in a common journey.

YOUR PERSONAL GUIDE

The journey toward living your soul's divine purpose is an ongoing process of self-discovery and increased awareness that provides new perspectives on life. *Getting Thru to Your Soul* brings this lofty subject down to earth, helping you to participate in this process more consciously, as you become your own source of divine light and wisdom. It is also a tool that counselors and therapists can use to understand more precisely how to help their clients through their challenges.

We will present Seven Spiritual Activations, which correspond to seven stages we all go through on the spiritual journey. This book also includes practical information on the human energy system and the changes it undergoes in the activation process. We support this information with state-of-the-art healing processes to speed you on your way. These processes can help you to access deeper levels of your awareness and integrate the vast understanding of your soul into your daily life.

What is the ultimate goal of the activations? In short, we are here to freely express the soul's joy in all aspects of our life. This is not the same thing as the concept of living happily ever after that we read about in fairy tales. People on the spiritual path do not solve all of their problems and live happily ever after without any further effort or conscious participation. Instead, the journey brings deeper meaning to life and allows us to see the challenges we face as opportunities to grow.

THE FOUR KEYS TO GETTING THRU TO YOUR SOUL

This book is divided into four parts, each focusing on one of the Four Keys to Getting Thru to Your Soul.

First Key: Understanding Your Soul

The first key is understanding the multi-dimensional realms of the soul, the soul's journey, and how your daily experiences relate to your spiritual awakening. This part of the book provides an overview of the journey, along with the seven stages and activations we all experience as we open to the power of the soul. Each stage involves completing lessons and developing higher levels of understanding that activate more of the soul's light and wisdom.

Second Key: Connecting with Your Soul's Reality

With an overview of the spiritual journey, you will be ready to establish a direct connection with your soul. When you encounter difficulties, this connection can become a resource for guidance. As a companion on your spiritual journey, your soul can provide a more profound way to experience life.

This part of the book also describes the human energy system, which reflects the soul's journey and purpose. It includes techniques to bring the system into balance, focusing on Spiritual Kinesiology, which is described later in this chapter. These methods can bring the healing power of the soul's wisdom and light to any issue and they are simple enough that you can start using them right away.

Third Key: Becoming an Expression of Your Soul

Here we provide details about the challenges each of us needs to overcome as we progress through the spiritual activations and become expressions of our souls. This part of the book includes more healing techniques that can help you to re-unify with your soul at each stage. The goal is to help you to progress through your lessons easily and with greater awareness. Since these lessons apply to people of all races, religious backgrounds, and national origins, their descriptions also provide an enlightening perspective on the condition of the human species and our evolutionary potential.

Fourth Key: Living Your Divine Purpose

This part of the book focuses on attaining the goal of the spiritual journey: living your divine purpose. The final activations take you to the point where you can integrate your soul's expression into all aspects of your life. Again, we include healing techniques to help you to identify and clear the blockages that stand between you and your goal.

Note: Along with describing the stages and the healing techniques, we present examples of the processes in action throughout the book. We have changed the names of the clients and students who participated in this way to preserve their privacy.

MASTERING THE HEALING TECHNIQUES

This book contains extensive information about the spiritual journey, along with leading-edge healing techniques and visualization processes to facilitate your progress. For the best results, we recommend reading the entire book while you start working with the first few processes. Each technique builds on the one before it, so using each one at least a few times will allow you to move to the next with confidence. Meanwhile, reading the whole book will give you an overview that will help you decide where you want to focus your attention further.

We have spent considerable time and energy developing the healing techniques we present in this book. Our goal is to help you advance on the spiritual path as quickly and easily as possible, which is what these techniques do. We view this book as a companion to our earlier one, *Getting Thru to Your Emotions with EFT*. The Emotional Freedom Techniques (EFT) and the Getting Thru Techniques (GTT) that were covered in that book are also powerful tools for your spiritual growth, so we will integrate some of those concepts and techniques with the information presented here.

The *Getting Thru to Your Soul* processes derive their power from their holistic focus. The term "holistic" refers to integrating all of the parts of the whole. This includes healing on the physical, emotional, mental, and spiritual levels. From this perspective, all true healing is spiritual healing, which is the highest level; and the soul is the most powerful healer.

With a holistic approach, any healing process is natural and organic. Along with expanding on the GTT techniques presented in *Getting Thru to Your Emotions with EFT*, this book provides more amazing techniques that you can use with virtually any kind of problem. These techniques focus on the use of guided visualization and kinesiology (muscle testing).

The Power of Visualization

The process of awakening connects you with higher dimensions of reality through the experience of your higher senses in dreams and visualization processes. These higher senses include your inner sight, inner feeling, inner hearing, and inner knowing. You may even experience smells and tastes in your visualizations. You can connect with these higher senses anytime by relaxing and releasing the control of the rational mind, so you can tap into the deeper levels of your awareness in the unconscious mind. This connection also allows you to access the higher dimensions of reality and your soul's wisdom.

The GTT techniques are based largely on the use of visualization. Whether this is a new experience or you feel completely comfortable with accessing your higher senses, these processes will help you to expand your awareness. You will learn to use visualization for personal transformation and to access the multi-dimensional awareness of your soul.

Your abilities to access your higher senses and your soul's awareness improve with practice. The GTT processes will help you to connect more and more powerfully with the energy of your soul, clear blockages, and increase the clarity of your higher senses. One of the main goals of this book is to establish a strong soul connection that will help you to approach your questions and challenges from a higher perspective. As previously mentioned, anchoring the expression of your soul into all aspects of your life is the ultimate goal.

Spiritual Kinesiology (SK)

Kinesiology refers to the use of muscle testing to access information from the unconscious mind and the body's innate intelligence. Many people consider it to be the most advanced diagnostic healing tool available today. It works by testing how the strength of a muscle is affected by focusing on a stimulus or a part of the body. In his groundbreaking book *Life Energy*, John Diamond, M.D., describes the effectiveness of kinesiology: "The power of the work is amazing, and the power of the body to crystallize these words and feelings into an instant response is absolutely marvelous."

Kinesiology may be used to test how the body is affected by

different substances, environmental factors, and verbal statements. There are now a number of approaches to kinesiology that are based on the work of Dr. George Goodheart, a chiropractor who developed Applied Kinesiology in the 1960s. Dr. Goodheart established a direct relationship between responses to different muscle movements and the functions of the body.

Since that time, the use of kinesiology has expanded into virtually all levels of healing. Dr. John Diamond, a psychotherapist in search of more effective techniques to use with his clients, developed Behavioral Kinesiology, which focuses on balancing the meridian system. Dr. Steven Paul Shepard simplified Goodheart's work in his book *Healing Energies*, which provides techniques that just about anyone can use to determine a person's health needs. Hypnotherapist Carl Carpenter integrated hypnotherapy and kinesiology into the amazingly simple and effective healing techniques that he calls Hypno-Kinesiology. These techniques, in turn, form the foundation for the Spiritual Kinesiology techniques we use in this book. We will refer to Spiritual Kinesiology as SK.

You can measure many things with kinesiology, including the muscle response to:

- Physical conditions
- Foods and supplements
- Emotional imbalances like fear, anger, and resentment
- Limiting beliefs and attitudes
- Problems with people, jobs, home, money
- Imbalances in the body's energy system

This book includes a variety of SK checklists that you can use to measure your progress in the different stages and aspects of the spiritual journey. These checklists will help you to pinpoint issues you need to address to take your next steps. The addition of the SK clearing techniques allows you to complete the process by releasing the blockages. These techniques are fast, easy-to-use, and non-invasive. If you are helping other people with them, receivers of SK do not have to go into the details of their problems to release the blockages. At the same time, they are fully aware of what is happening and often gain profound insights.

Emotional Freedom Techniques (EFT)

This book also includes the option of using EFT to clear the blockages that kinesiology and the GTT processes reveal. EFT is based on a series of discoveries that some psychologists consider to be among the most important breakthroughs in their field in the twentieth century. It includes a group of amazingly fast and effective techniques that just about anyone can use to overcome all kinds of troubling emotions and more.

We use EFT regularly with our clients and ourselves. These techniques are so effective that some call them a modern miracle. EFT works by tapping on a series of acupuncture points on the meridian system to release energetic blockages. No special knowledge is required to use the techniques, so they are rapidly gaining popularity. For those who already use EFT, we will include references in this book to ways that you can use these techniques with the processes we present.

Those who are new to EFT will find an introduction in Appendix C. This appendix explains how to use the most basic EFT technique, the Short Sequence, which works most of the time. You may also want to obtain a copy of *Getting Thru to Your Emotions with EFT* to accompany this book.

MORE HELP WITH GETTING THRU

In our descriptions of the techniques in this book, we have tried to be thorough and to provide as much information as possible. Some people may understand the techniques better by also seeing them in action and hearing then presented, so we have also produced three video tapes and two audio cassette tapes to accompany this book. These materials are designed to accelerate your comprehension and your ability to benefit from the extensive information presented here.

The Video Tapes

On the videos, we demonstrate each of the techniques, using real-life examples of Spiritual Kinesiology and the Getting Thru Techniques in action. These professionally produced tapes help to clarify the mechanics of muscle testing and the nuts and bolts of each of the methods. They also complement the book by providing step-by-step instructions on how to do all of the processes. We highly recommend them to anyone who wants to master these techniques.

The Audio Tapes

The audio tapes are guided versions of the Getting Thru Techniques with background music that allow you to relax and experience the processes. They are designed for people who find listening to the guided visualization processes easier than reading through them in the book.

Clairvoyant Skills for Getting Thru to Your Soul

The development of your intuitive and clairvoyant skills is an integral part of the spiritual journey. Most of the people we work with expect these skills to simply appear in their lives, but this is not how it works. It is actually very much like learning a new language; the more you practice, the more proficient you become. This tape series will help you develop these skills using the techniques we have learned and developed on our own spiritual journeys and in our work with others. We present the techniques in audiocassette format, so you can experiment with using them as you listen. A short manual that outlines the program and illustrates the techniques accompanies the tapes.

You can find more information about the videos, the audio tapes, and the clairvoyant techniques in Appendix D.

INVOLVING FRIENDS

A supportive friend or group of friends can be invaluable in your awakening. You can help each other to stay focused and learn from your experiences together. These interactions may also serve as a model for cultivating spiritual friendships.

Guiding others through the visualization techniques can be enlightening for all involved. You can read the process while the other person goes through it, and facilitate the use of Spiritual Kinesiology or EFT as required for clearing. You just need to adjust the wording a bit as you go along, because the processes in this book are designed to be read by the user.

TAKING CONTROL OF YOUR LIFE

Before presenting the SK, EFT, and GTT techniques, we want to let you know that you are in control. Like coaches, we are available to teach you effective methods for helping yourself. You are free to progress in your own way and at your own pace.

The purpose of this book is to help you release the blockages that prevent you from fully embracing your soul, and to help you heal them holistically. We are not licensed psychologists or medical health professionals. We are Ministers of Holistic Healing and serve others as spiritual counselors and teachers. As such, we do not recommend substituting the technique we present for the professional services of doctors, psychologists, and psychiatrists. We advise you to have their permission before using any of these techniques.

Fortunately, the techniques we present are practically risk-free. However, that does not mean you will not have a problem using them. You or someone you help with these techniques may be an exception. As we are sure you can appreciate, we will not assume responsibility in this regard. The responsibility for your spiritual, mental, emotional, and physical well-being must rest with you. We likewise hand the responsibility for the use of the techniques in this book over to you.

We conclude with the following statements, which we pass on as our agreement with you, our readers. We ask you to:

- Take complete responsibility for your spiritual, mental, emotional, and/or physical well-being.

- Instruct others whom you help with the techniques we present in this book to take complete responsibility for their spiritual, mental, emotional, and/or physical well-being.

- Agree to hold harmless Phillip Mountrose, Jane Mountrose, and anyone involved with the Emotional Freedom Techniques, Spiritual Kinesiology, and the Getting Thru Techniques from any claims made by anyone whom you seek to help with EFT, SK, and GTT.

- Use these techniques under the supervision of a qualified psychologist or physician. Don't use these techniques to try to solve a problem where your common sense would tell you it is not appropriate.

If you are not able to agree with these statements, please do not read further, and do not use the techniques in this book.

1st Key

UNDERSTANDING
YOUR SOUL

CHAPTER ONE
The Path of
Spiritual Awakening

Within man is the soul of the whole,
the wise silence, the universal beauty,
to which every part and particle is equally related,
the eternal One.

–RALPH WALDO EMERSON

Reflecting on the meaning of life and the existence of the soul is an awe-inspiring venture. Who are we? And why are we here? These are some of life's most perplexing questions. Life is different for each of us, but there are common threads that have woven their way through all the cultures of humanity and unite us in a common journey.

From the earliest time in our recorded history, spiritual traditions sprouted up in primitive cultures all around the world. The common thread in these traditions is their holistic view. Everything from animals, birds, and plants to the ground we walk on, the oceans, the mountains, and even the air we breathe are considered to be alive and connected by a unifying spirit. All are one and one is all. And everything has significance and meaning.

With the development of our contemporary religious structure, industrialization, and modernization, these spiritual traditions were eliminated in favor of a more scientific approach. Science and technology have improved our lives us in innumerable ways, but they have also narrowed our vision. We have lost sight of the connectedness of all things, along with our relationships with our souls.

Through the eyes of science, we have been compartmentalized into separate pieces. Most doctors view our physical bodies as operating independently of our emotions and thoughts, and deny the spirit altogether. Similarly, psychologists and counselors analyze our thoughts and feelings as operating independently of our bodies and souls. And our spiritual leaders are expected to oversee our spiritual well-being without interfering with the realms of psychologists and doctors. Scientists look at the external world of the five normal senses without considering the importance of the multi-dimensional world that exists within ourselves.

We sense that there is more to explore; that behind our tangible world there is another level of reality with deeper significance.

Science and technology are advancing at an amazing rate. The pace of life has also quickened, and individual wealth has grown, along with our appetites for the trappings of success. These external rewards have provided the illusion of progress, but have left a deep emptiness within. As we move faster and suffer from the related stress and anxiety, we find ourselves looking beyond our normal perspectives into the unknown. We can see that our externally oriented society is not taking us where we want to go. A new outfit, car, or home will not fill the void we find within ourselves. We are connecting with the guiding light of the soul.

THE LIGHT OF THE SOUL

As you will see, the soul's guiding light is easy to detect. It is directly linked with the energy that sustains life. Your greatest joy and excitement are also indicators of your soul's divine purpose, which makes you feel profoundly alive. What brings you the greatest joy? What would you do with your life if you had no limits of time or money? Is there anything you would like to do to help other people and the planet?

All of these questions evoke your soul's presence, because achieving more joy, love, and freedom are part of your soul's purpose. Focusing on making these positive states a reality is a key to progressing on the spiritual journey. Conversely, stifling your joy and excitement diminishes your life energy and slows your evolution. This is why so many people face depression. In the United States, as many as one in five women and one in ten men fight depression at some time in their lives.

Here is another important question. Do you believe that you can have a life filled with joy, love, and freedom, where you can play a role in bettering society? If not, what is stopping you? It is common to have doubts, but, sooner or later, a loving and joyful life is where your soul's journey will lead.

THE CONTINUUMS OF CHANGE

Recognizing and freely expressing your soul's divine purpose is the ultimate goal of the spiritual journey, but there is much more to it than that. Since we are multi-faceted or multi-dimensional, there are a number of ways to measure our progress along the way. Figure 1.1 shows some of these gauges as The Continuums of Change. Each continuum provides a piece of the puzzle of who we are and where we are going. As we progress on the path, we gradually release more of the limiting qualities that are listed on the left sides of the continuums and

FIGURE 1.1
THE CONTINUUMS OF CHANGE

This is how the spiritual journey affects different aspects of life.

RELATIONSHIP WITH THE SOUL
From ego in charge . . . . to soul in charge

ENERGY FIELD
From darkness, small aura . . . . to lightness, large aura

CONSCIOUS AWARENESS
From mostly unconscious . . . . to mostly conscious

LOVE
From judgment . . . . to acceptance

RELATIONSHIPS
From co-dependency . . . . to sovereignty

POWER
From false external power . . . . to true internal power

CONSCIENCE
From not responsible for actions . . . . to fully responsible for actions

EMOTIONAL AWARENESS
From insensitive to feelings . . . . to sensitive to feelings

DEPENDABILITY
From emotionally unreliable . . . . to emotionally reliable

TRUTH
From subjective truth of ego . . . . to objective truth of soul

TRUST
From fear of harm . . . . to trust in divine order

WILL
From indecision . . . . to right action

integrate more of the expansive qualities on the right sides of the continuums. Here is a summary of each one:

- **Relationship with the Soul:** The spiritual journey leads each of us from the false self to the true self, from the wounded ego to the soul. While the wounded ego's focus is on outward show ("keeping up with the Jones'), the soul brings a new focus on inner fulfillment.

- **Energy Field:** The spiritual journey also takes us from darkness to light. As we travel down the road of life, learning lessons and releasing blockages to embracing our soul and our divine purpose, more spiritual light flows through the physical body and the surrounding energy field or aura. In our clairvoyant counseling work, the first gauge we use to measure a person's progress is the amount of light the energy field holds. This "light quotient" provides an accurate measurement of where an individual is on the path.

- **Conscious Awareness:** At the beginning of the journey, we are largely unconscious and our decisions are mostly based on programming in the unconscious mind. This generally leaves a wide gap between our daily awareness and our soul awareness. In this state, we can easily forget the goal of remembering the soul for days or weeks at a time. As the journey progresses, our daily awareness and our soul awareness come closer and closer together. We remember the soul more frequently and feel its energy integrating into our daily activities.

- **Love:** To the wounded ego, love usually comes with conditions. It is also laced with judgment, which ultimately relates to the ego's low self-esteem. The soul loves unconditionally, accepting ourselves and others as we are.

- **Relationships:** The ego generally becomes immersed in dependence on others for one's sense of self. The soul shifts the focus to achieving a state of energetic sovereignty that allows us to honor both ourselves and others.

- **Power:** The ego's concept of power depends on an outward show of force, while the soul brings us the true internal power we need to live our divine purpose.

- **Conscience:** The wounding of the ego is accompanied by an inability to take responsibility for oneself. The soul brings an awareness of how our actions affect those around us and takes full responsibility for these actions.

- **Emotional Awareness:** The ego's low level of conscious awareness is understandably accompanied by a lack of emotional sensitivity, both toward oneself and others. As our conscious awareness grows, we also become more sensitive to what is occurring emotionally within ourselves and others.

- **Dependability:** With a low level of awareness of our feelings and how their inappropriate expression can hurt those around us, we may be unaware of the importance of being emotionally reliable. The soul's emergence brings an ability to express our feelings in a way that honors all concerned.

- **Truth:** The ego is cut off from the wisdom of the soul, so its sense of truth is often misguided and accompanied by misunderstanding of others. As the ego and the soul unite in a cooperative relationship, the soul's truth comes through, accompanied by understanding of the perspectives of others as well.

- **Trust:** The ego is often immersed in fear of harm and threatened by the challenges that life inevitably brings. The emerging energy of the soul brings a balanced sense of trust in the divine order of life and a willingness to explore the unknown.

- **Will:** The ego, which has been fragmented by the difficult experiences of the past, may be unable to muster the will that is needed to maintain one's direction in the face of adversity. As the fragmentation of the ego is replaced by the unity of the soul, we develop will and a sense of right action.

As overviews of the evolutionary process, the continuums provide some food for thought. We will also describe soul development as a healing process, as we heal the wounded parts of ourselves who have cut us off from the soul. In her mind opening book *Hands of Light*, Barbara Ann Brennan, a pioneer in energy healing, describes healing as a process of "remembering who you are. Within the aura the process of healing is a process that rebalances the energies in each body [we will discuss these 'bodies,' which represent different levels of our awareness, in later chapters]. When all the energies in each body are balanced, health occurs. The soul has learned its particular lesson and, therefore, has more cosmic truth."

CREATING JOY

Most people do not realize how important happiness is. You can start to manifest more of your soul's purpose by including more joyful activities in each day. These small changes may seem insignificant at first, but the seeds you plant germinate, and over time you will find that you are able to expand on them more and more.

Tibet's Dalai Lama, one of the world's foremost spiritual leaders, describes the attainment of happiness as the purpose of life. At first glance, this may seem selfish. But, on closer examination, it makes sense. Happy people tend to be more open, sociable, creative, and flexible. They also have a greater ability to reach out and help others than unhappy people, who tend to be more self-centered and withdrawn.

Being joyful is a way to help both yourself and others.

Here is how the Dalai Lama suggests reaching this goal in his book *The Art of Happiness*: "One begins by identifying those factors which lead to happiness and those factors which lead to suffering. Having done this, one then sets about gradually eliminating those factors which lead to suffering and cultivating those which lead to happiness."

Studies show that simply focusing on positive feelings like joy and gratitude makes a difference. A local newspaper article described a study conducted at the University of California at Davis. One of the professors wanted to test the effects of focusing on positive things. He divided his class of two hundred students into three groups. During each of the following ten weeks, the first group was asked to make a list of five things they were grateful for. The second group was asked to write down five things they found irritating. The third group was asked to simply list five major events of the week.

At the end of the ten weeks, the students were all asked how they felt about their lives and how they felt physically, among other things. Overall, the first group reported feeling better than before. They also felt happier overall than either of the other groups and showed less symptoms of physical illness. Interestingly, the group that focused on major events tended to list negative events more than positive ones and had results that were similar to the group that focused on irritations.

KEEPING A JOY JOURNAL

Keeping a joy journal can help you to cultivate happiness. It is also a wonderful way to open to the unlimited possibilities of the soul. Write down what comes into your mind when you ask yourself a question like the one at the beginning of this chapter: If you did not have any limits of time, money, location, or anything else that limits you now, what would bring you the most joy and fulfillment? There may be some big things and some small things. There may be some things you have wanted to do for many years or that you used to do when you were younger. There may be some things you have thought about, but haven't taken that final step of including them in your life.

There may be some things you long to do to help others.

Money is a subject we all need to address. The idea that money creates happiness is one of our society's great myths. When people want more of it, they are usually expecting that the money will bring them something else. If you think money will solve your problems, ask yourself what it would provide. Some common answers are increased security, less stress, more fun, and greater freedom. Understanding what you really want can help, because money alone is usually not the solution. In many cases, money has little or nothing to do with it.

We have helped many people to connect with their soul's purpose and have noticed that there are usually some simple steps that they can take that do not necessitate making major changes. One example is a lovely woman we will call Elaine, who received some counseling from Jane. Elaine enjoyed singing until she married a controlling man who was critical of the sound of her voice. She stopped singing then and had missed it ever since. At the time she spoke with Jane, Elaine had left this relationship and was living alone. She could do as she pleased, but had not started singing again, even though the thought frequently entered her mind.

This may seem like a small thing, but singing is an aspect of Elaine's soul expression. If she withholds that expression from her life, she is denying a part of her soul and her true joy. Instead she is unwittingly strengthening her wounded ego, which often resists taking such steps toward soul expression out of fear of losing its control. To shift the balance, it is important to bring your soul's expression into your reality by doing things that bring you joy.

Some of your soul's desires may not manifest so quickly. In such cases, you can approach them incrementally. In this regard, intent is much more powerful than you may realize. You just start by making small shifts in the direction that your soul's joy is guiding you. We have done this ourselves with amazing success. For example, we realized a while ago that we enjoyed traveling and wanted to see more of the world. We could not stop everything we were doing right then and see the world, but we started focusing on traveling more. Now traveling has become an integral part of our work and our souls' joy.

Living your soul's purpose may also involve making difficult decisions that shake the foundation of your reality. If you are in personal or business relationships that limit your joyful expression, you may need to make some major changes. As you move into your soul's expression, you deserve to be surrounded by people who nurture your development and encourage the emergence of your divine purpose. You would not be here, and your soul would not have its desires if you were not intended to manifest them. By looking carefully, though, you will notice that there is often a fine line between a desire to express the joy of the soul and a desire to relieve the pain or fear of the ego. You need to look deeply within for your truth. This book will help you in your search.

To understand the multi-dimensional reality of the soul, we will provide some background on the essence and significance of the spiritual journey. We begin with three questions. What is our reality? How does it function? And who are we really?

THE NATURE OF OUR REALITY

Even though people commonly refer to living in the third dimension, they rarely question what this means. Most people understand our reality as the only possible form of existence. With 100 billion stars in the Milky Way Galaxy and 100 billion galaxies beyond, this seems unlikely. We regard our third dimensional reality as a perspective on life. Since we are multi-dimensional, we have access to other perspectives and other dimensions. In this life, we have chosen to explore this one.

In the third dimension, we live with limitations imposed upon us by our thinking. We can transcend these limits by seeking a more tangible connection with our souls and the spiritual realms. With this in mind, a holistic approach is actually a multi-dimensional approach, as it acknowledges the existence of different perspectives. We see that we are more than a mind and a body. We are spiritual beings with many levels of awareness that we can access at will if we know how.

Of course, reaching this understanding can take time. For many years, we both recall feeling like insignificant cogs in the wheels that moved our society forward. We somehow sensed that there was more to life, but we felt that we could not have any meaningful impact on the direction the world was moving in. We both grew up in the 1950s in the midst of fallout shelters and predictions of an untimely end to life as we knew it. We were not sure if we would ever reach adulthood.

But years passed, and we were still here. As young adults, we faced the uncertainty that characterizes many people in our society today. We did not know how we could be of value or how we fit into the larger picture of humanity. We finally recognized that every individual is important and that each of us has an impact on the world whether we realize it or not. We are expressing our choices for the kind of world we want to create each day in the things we say, the ways we treat others, the things we choose to spend our money on, and so on. But for those who feel powerless in this complex world, these choices are being made in the absence of conscious intent, without any recognition of the impact each person has on the whole.

Fortunately, this is beginning to change. As we connect more with our souls, we begin to make more conscious decisions and more positive contributions to the world.

HOW OUR REALITY WORKS

Our spiritual traditions provide valuable clues to the multidimensional realms of the soul. From the soul's viewpoint, everything is connected, and all the events of our lives have an underlying meaning and purpose. While the prevailing scientific perspective regards life as a series of random events, there is a divine order underlying all of our experiences.

Carl Jung recognized this divine order in his exploration of synchronicity, which could be described as the science of meaningful coincidences. From this perspective, the outer world is actually a reflection of the soul's journey. We are here to learn from the situations that come up and the people we meet. When we look at life this way, it becomes a mysterious and magical experience. The challenges we face become gifts that allow our souls to grow and evolve. We may not welcome all of these gifts immediately, but we definitely have the opportunity to understand our lives in a more profound way.

Interestingly enough, the concepts of synchronicity are finding validation in the emerging science of quantum physics, which helps to complete the picture. Through quantum physics, scientists have recognized that everything is energy, and through this energy, everything is connected. Our consciousness actually affects the energy. We have all noticed how people attract different types of experiences to themselves. Take the example of a woman who is accident-prone. Energetically, she may be like an accident waiting to happen. You probably wouldn't want to ride in a car with her. On the other hand, a man who believes that people are basically good consistently attracts positive interactions to himself.

OUR TRUE SPIRITUAL IDENTITIES

Quantum physics shows us that everything is energy. In reality, we are energetic beings of light who have created physical bodies as reflections of our true divine selves. Our unique energetic frequencies determine how each of us experiences our environment. This is how those of us who have developed our clairvoyant skills can "read" people; we use our multi-dimensional awareness to perceive the fields of energy that define our bodies and our reality.

Multi-dimensionally, the oversoul or higher self is the true eternal self who exists in higher realms or levels of reality beyond this one. Understanding that all of life is connected, this higher aspect of the soul exists in a joyful and loving state. Unfortunately, most of us do not recognize our souls as our true selves, because we have blockages in our minds and energy fields that prevent us from seeing clearly, much like having filters over our eyes that cut off the light. These are the limitations of the five physical senses, which connect us with third dimensional reality.

Actually, there is much more to life; new worlds unfold as we learn to connect with our multi-dimensional selves through our higher senses, which include our inner feeling, inner vision, inner hearing, and inner knowing.

As we learn to expand our awareness beyond our normal senses and open to our multi-dimensional selves, we can access the light and wisdom of the soul.

This soul connection then allows us to begin to release the energetic blockages that limit us. Gradually, the filters are removed, and the light becomes clearer and clearer. We connect more with the light of the soul, and our physical reality changes as a reflection.

With all of this in mind, we can see more clearly how synchronicity works. Our physical bodies, auras, and experiences all reflect the stages of our soul's journey and the lessons we need to learn. While our egos generally avoid bringing awareness to our difficulties, our souls guide us to recognize the challenges we need to face to move toward genuine fulfillment.

All of this happens in a perfect order. As we move forward on the path, we attract more light to ourselves. This light provides a deeper understanding of our reality; it also shines on dark spots or blockages, so we can examine them, clear them, and learn more about ourselves. These exposed blockages may bring problems like physical pain or illness, accidents, disturbing emotions, and conflicts with others. Resolving these problems by clearing the blockages allows us to progress further, so that we can be more present in each moment and experience life in a more conscious and fulfilling way.

By contrast, not dealing with the problems we face sends the blockages deeper into our energy systems and finally into our physical bodies, where we ultimately experience discomfort or illness. Each blockage also takes energy to maintain, and allowing them to build up can leave us feeling depleted and dissatisfied with life.

THE PURPOSE OF THE SPIRITUAL JOURNEY

To the soul, nothing is accidental. We came here to learn and evolve. The goal is to reawaken to the reality of the soul and to experience oneness with God and all of life. As Ghandi so aptly stated, "God resides in every human form and in every particle of his creation." This connection allows us to participate in or to co-create with the divine plan for humanity.

But how did we get into this state of forgetting? When we became physical, we lost sight of our true identities. Psychologically, we moved from a state of conscious awareness to a state of unconsciousness. Spiritually, we lost the ability to recognize the soul as the source of light and guidance. In the process, our higher senses shut down, leaving us limited to the third dimensional experience of the normal five senses.

To help us maneuver within this reality, each of us has a personality or ego. The ego helps us to deal with the third dimension, preferably under the guidance of the soul. But this relationship is generally reversed. In an attempt to cope with life's challenges, and through continuous exposure to negativity and limiting beliefs, the ego usually takes command and becomes disconnected from the soul. The ego then views the limitations of the personality and the three-dimensional world of our five senses as its only identity.

We refer to the ego in this disconnected state as the wounded ego or false personality. Identifying with the wounded ego corresponds with developing blockages to our awareness, extinguishing the light of the soul. The ego does its best, but it cannot see the big picture and guide us toward a loving and joyful life. In the absence of the soul's overview, the ego becomes fragmented and immersed in fear. This is usually so extreme that the ego even fears yielding its dominant position to the soul. It perceives the emergence of the soul as its death and throws up roadblocks on the spiritual path.

Part of the journey, then, is a battle between different parts of oneself. Gradually this conflict subsides, as the ego recognizes that the soul actually wants to progress hand-in-hand with the ego. So as we respond to our inner longing to bring more meaning to life and return to wholeness, the ego takes its rightful position as an intermediary between the soul and the outside world. We refer to the ego that has been transformed in this way as the healthy ego or true personality.

Figure 1.2 is an Overview of the Spiritual Journey that shows how the relationship between the ego and the soul changes in the process. As we progress, we also become more connected with the earth and all forms of life. The grounding cord on the diagrams shows how this relationship strengthens as we awaken to the soul.

THE HIGHER REALMS

The spiritual journey sounds like a long one, and, of course, it is. Fortunately, we are not alone. Many have gone before us and reach to us from the higher realms. These invisible beings of light, which include our guides, the ascended masters, and the angels, watch over us and keep us on track. They clear the path and provide us with the tools we need along the way. On a larger scale, they are orchestrating a divine plan for humanity,

FIGURE 1.2
OVERVIEW OF THE SPIRITUAL JOURNEY

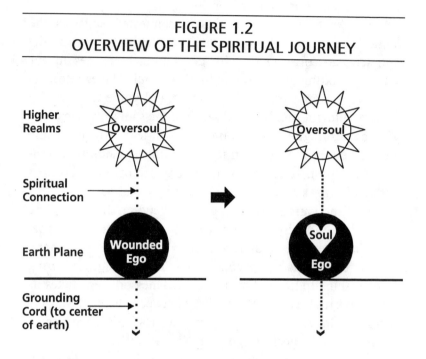

When the journey begins, the oversoul, the higher aspect of the soul in the higher realms, and the ego on the physical plane are separate. The wounded ego is alone in the dark, with little of the soul's light and wisdom to draw upon for guidance. The spiritual connection is weak, as is the grounding cord, and it is difficult for the individual to be in the present moment.

As one begins to progress on the path, the spiritual connection becomes stronger and the soul's energy starts to come down from the oversoul into the body, where it rests in the heart. The darkness of the wounded ego begins to yield to the love and light of the soul, which gradually becomes a genuine presence in one's life. The grounding cord also becomes stronger, providing more stability.

FIGURE 1.2
CONTINUED

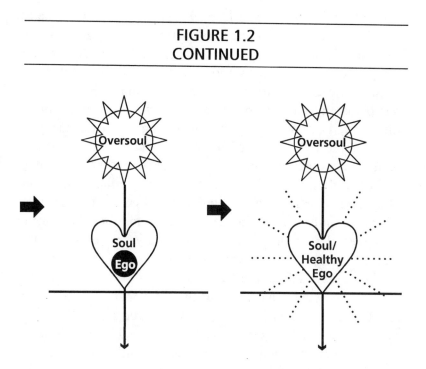

Further along on the journey, the spiritual connection becomes strong enough to create a direct connection between the oversoul and the body. The healing ego begins to align with the light and wisdom of the soul until the soul displaces the ego as the main guiding force in one's life. Grounding also becomes more secure, so the individual feels more comfortable in the body and in present time.

Finally, the soul and the now healthy ego combine their efforts with the goal of living one's divine purpose. The soul's awareness stabilizes in the body and the soul's light begins to radiate the frequency of co-creation. This allows one to live the soul's purpose with an understanding of what one is here to do. At this point, both the spiritual connection and the grounding cord are strong and secure.

and each of us has a role to play. Magically, we are exactly where we need to be to play this part. One of the goals of the spiritual journey is to connect with the higher realms, so we can participate consciously and co-create in the divine plan.

We believe that those of us who choose to move forward on our paths and embrace our purposes have a unique opportunity now, because society is undergoing dramatic changes. Most people are unaware of the spiritual activations, but many of us are awakening spiritually as society reaches toward a higher level of reality. Because of this acceleration, in a period of months or years, we can progress as far as we could have in a whole lifetime or more in the past. And for those who have been meandering on the spiritual path for years, those who are joining us now can conceivably achieve as much in a month as we did in years a decade or two ago.

We also believe that many of the rules that applied to our spiritual development in the past no longer apply. We have more options. While some may feel the need to withdraw to remote caves and monasteries to achieve enlightenment, you may feel guided to follow your path amidst the hustle and bustle of modern life, or somewhere in between. For the purposes of the divine plan, we believe that the goal is to infuse all parts of society with the light of our souls.

As you become lighter, your simple presence becomes a positive force wherever you go.

Of course, some people are resisting the changes. The violence we find in our society is the creation those who identify with the darkness and their wounded egos. Fortunately, many others are embracing the light and helping humanity to attain higher levels of awareness, bringing issues out of the darkness so we can all confront them. The fall of Communism is a powerful example of humanity's collective ability to generate change. Worldwide attention to subjects such as abuse and equal rights are further indications that we are evolving and attracting more light. They also mirror the dramatic changes so many of us are experiencing within ourselves.

EXPLORING THE MYSTERIES WITHIN

To understand the soul, we have to open to the mysteries within ourselves by connecting with the unconscious mind. Through this connection, we can systematically release our limitations and integrate more understanding of our true divine purpose. However, entering these realms is a foreign idea to many people. Our society as a whole has become enthralled by the progress of science and technology, cutting itself off from the spiritual realms. In a synchronous way, many individuals have grown accustomed to focusing exclusively on the elusive riches of the external world, cutting themselves off from the vast resources within themselves.

Current scientific and spiritual perspectives are generally very different. Through the validation of our five normal senses, science and technology are helping us to accomplish more in our outer world. Exploring the world of the soul requires us to look beyond these normal perceptions. We have to reach more deeply within ourselves for greater levels of awareness and learn to measure our accomplishments in terms of inner fulfillment.

Many people, like ourselves, view our time as one of transformation for all of humanity. We are being challenged to let go of our limited perspective on life and reach for a higher level of reality. In his book *Seat of the Soul*, Gary Zukav describes how we transcend the limitations of the physical senses to the experience of the higher senses. Opening to these higher senses allows us to see beyond the limitations of the third dimension into the higher realms. From this new point-of-view, we can understand how our current reality fits into the larger picture and how our higher senses help us evolve both as individuals and as a species.

Along with reflecting our normal senses and our higher senses, the scientific and spiritual approaches reflect our active and receptive sides, which are mirrored in the two halves of the brain. The left half of the brain represents the rational masculine side of our nature and the personality; it focuses on achievement. The right brain represents the receptive feminine side of our nature and the realms of the spirit; it focuses on inner fulfillment. Together these two windows on the world provide a complete picture of our identities as human beings.

Unfortunately, in our externally-oriented society, the spiritual, feminine side of our nature is generally ignored and undervalued. We have moved rapidly forward technologically, but fallen behind in understanding our true identities. U.S. workers have been called "world class workaholics," having an increasingly long work-week that surpasses all other advanced industrialized nations. As a result, many people are suffering from rising stress levels as they seek to fit more and more activities into each day. Others fall into depression, because they have no way to fill the emptiness they sense within themselves. Some become lost in addictions or turn to violence out of their inability to deal with the frustrations of modern life.

HUMANITY'S NEXT STEP

As mentioned earlier, this focus on outward achievement is starting to change as increasing numbers of individuals follow their inner longings to bring balance and meaning to their lives. More and more people are recognizing that the trappings of success do not bring fulfillment. Many are choosing quality of life over financial gain. We are preparing to take the next step in human development. It is in the balance of the active, externally oriented masculine and the receptive, spiritually-oriented feminine sides of our nature that we will find wholeness. Figure 1.3 provides a list of some of the characteristics that are associated with the right and left sides of the brain.

FIGURE 1.3
THE RIGHT AND LEFT SIDES OF THE BRAIN

LEFT	RIGHT
Masculine	Feminine
Activity	Receptivity
Domination	Nurturing
Activity	Being
Willing	Accepting
Organization	Creativity
Rational thought	Intuition
Competing	Sharing
Deduction	Having insight

The desire to create inner balance is part of human nature. Regardless, turning within and stepping onto the spiritual path can be frightening. Many people are afraid that below the surface of their awareness they will find terrible things that they will not be able to handle. Fortunately, our experience has consistently shown us that this is not the case. Those who are willing to take an honest look find the opposite. They discover that they have been limiting themselves by carrying unnecessary loads. Their true identities are much more beautiful, wonderful, and unique than they ever dared to imagine.

One time Jane had a dream that exemplified the fears and doubts many people experience. In the dream, she was out in the country, preparing to head home. She had a choice of two routes. The first, the main road, was where most of the people were traveling. This was like the freeway of life. It was smooth, relatively straight, and wide enough for cars to drive on easily. She could see quite a ways down the road, and it wasn't too interesting, but it was safe and well traveled. The other route was a narrow footpath, and Jane couldn't see very far ahead on it. Nevertheless, it looked much more interesting. It started by rising up a steep hillside leading into unfamiliar country on the other side. This, of course, was the spiritual path. The hill was covered with snow and ice; a few people were playing there, throwing snowballs, and enjoying themselves.

Jane chose to follow the footpath and started up the snowy slope. She got about half way up the hill, but could not reach the top, because she kept slipping on the ice. She finally gave up in frustration and never saw what was on the other side.

The next day, the dream kept coming into Jane's mind, so she knew she should explore it further. Using a dream analysis process, she recreated the scene on the icy hill in her mind and re-entered the dream. This time she noticed that she was carrying a heavy backpack. She knew that the hill represented her soul's path and that something was holding her back. Then it occurred to Jane that she was working steadfastly to carry the backpack, but she didn't even know what was inside. She simply assumed that she had to carry it. She pulled it over her shoulders, and when she open it up, she saw that it was full of ominous-looking dark, ugly, wiggling worms and bugs.

Examining them more closely, Jane recognized that they represented the parts of her life that were not fulfilling, parts that had become dark and ominous. She had been afraid to let go of them, because they were familiar and made her feel secure, like she was carrying an important load. She was amazed that she had carried them religiously for so long, and once she could see them for what they really were, the solution was simple. She took off the backpack, relieved to be free of those ugly squirmy things, and set it aside. Now Jane continued easily to the top and beyond, into a place of great peace and beauty.

At one time or another, most of us find ourselves on roads that do not seem to go anywhere, burdened by heavy loads that we do not need to carry. Soul awakening involves letting go of those loads and moving into that place of peace and beauty within oneself.

Another revealing note on the dream: Once Jane got to the other side of the hill, she noticed that Phillip was walking with her. He had been there the whole time, but Jane was so absorbed in what she was doing that she didn't notice him. She had felt that she had to carry the load alone, not recognizing that Phillip was willing to assist her. Many people, like Jane, assume that they have to carry the entire load alone, not realizing that others are there to provide support along the way. The soul's journey is an individual one and may seem lonely at times, but when we look around, we will generally find the support we need to help us to move forward and provide companionship along the way.

THE EMERGENCE OF AWARENESS

We have discussed how each of us unconsciously views life and how our reality reflects this perspective. With the development of energetic blockages, the unconscious mind controls almost everything we do. Regardless, the conscious mind, which is generally ruled by the wounded ego, thinks that it is in control. Awareness provides a meaningful gauge of one's spiritual development. In most people, the conscious mind represents 10 percent or less of their potential awareness. The other 90 percent is concealed below the surface in the unconscious mind. When this is the case, the unconscious mind is operating independently, with little or no awareness on our parts.

You may be wondering why the soul would volunteer to come into this state of unconsciousness. Why can't we just be connected with all that is and live in a continuous state of joy, love, and freedom? This is, of course, what we are aiming for. But, looking at the purpose of life, it is by learning from our experiences that we build depth of character and reconnect with our true selves. In the process, we become more loving, resourceful, and compassionate.

To summarize, as we have descended to the physical plane and submerged ourselves in darkness, we have thrown the things we could not integrate into the unconscious mind, which may represent as much as 90 percent of the mind. In this condition, we are almost totally immersed in the physical plane and the ego with little light to guide us. The soul only plays a minor role, if any.

As we return to wholeness, we gradually integrate all of those unconscious patterns until the percentages become reversed. We are aware of ourselves and our spiritual paths. The wounded ego has been healed and yielded its control to the soul's dominion. We are largely conscious, with a small unconscious element that gives us time to integrate our experiences.

SUSPENDING JUDGMENT

As we understand that we are synchronously attracting our experiences and notice that challenges tend to replay in our lives, there may be a tendency to judge ourselves for the weaknesses we perceive. Similarly, in the medical community, an illness that is perceived to have a psychological component is seen as a sign of weakness. This is not an accurate assessment. When we attract experiences to ourselves, it simply means that there are some things we can learn from them.

We need to start by suspending judgment. These limiting feelings hide the truth. Holistically, every symptom has a physical, emotional, mental, and spiritual component, because everything is connected. We will describe these components in detail, because understanding the relationships between them is part of the spiritual journey. For now, it may help to know that on the spiritual level, each lesson increases our understanding of how magnificent we are. This awareness grows as we progress through the spiritual activations, which are the subject of the next chapter.

CHAPTER TWO
The Seven Spiritual Activations

We are born into the world of nature;
our second birth is into the world of spirit.

–BHAGAVAD-GITA

Whether you are just developing a relationship with your soul or have been on the spiritual path for some time, it is normal to wonder how you are progressing. We struggled with this question ourselves for many years. Then, as our higher senses opened, we began to perceive the movement from darkness to light and other incremental shifts that we explored in The Continuums of Change in Figure 1.1.

Through our studies and experiences with clients and students, we have since developed a roadmap for the spiritual path. The journey of connecting with the soul and embracing one's divine purpose takes each of us through a series of spiritual activations, which correspond to stages of exploring different parts of our inner and outer worlds. The completion of each stage is accompanied by a noticeable boost in spiritual awareness, light, and wisdom that mark the activation. You can probably recall a time when you suddenly broke through the challenges you were dealing with and experienced a new level of understanding and spiritual presence. This breakthrough was probably an activation, which marked your graduation to the next stage in your spiritual development.

We now recognize seven stages and major spiritual activations that we all experience in the process of awakening. The timing of when we step onto the spiritual path, how far we go, and how quickly we progress all relate to our soul's purpose. Wherever we are in the process, each one of us is in the right place. It is something like being in a time-release capsule. When it is time to awaken, the journey begins.

Many people have dreams about being in school that relate to their spiritual journeys. Phillip periodically dreamed that he was in college. In these dreams, he would inevitably get lost, feeling unprepared, not knowing his schedule, and missing his classes. They left him feeling disturbed and unfulfilled.

Then Phillip had another dream. He was in college, as usual, enrolling in more classes. He was again uncertain about where to go and where he would be staying. This time, he found his class schedule and a dormitory to stay in. He learned that the dormitory was just a temporary one and that he would be moving soon. At first this disturbed Phillip. He had that unsettled feeling, as if he was again unprepared and everything was tentative and shifting. But this time, something changed. Phillip realized that things were fine; he was where he was supposed to be. He felt a great relief as he accepted the transitory nature of life. Everything was just temporary anyway.

After waking, Phillip realized that this dream college was his Hall of Learning, where he received the higher learning of his soul. He knew he could let go of his fears and trust in himself and the future. He was as prepared as he needed to be, and there was nothing to worry about. He might as well enjoy the courses as he continued on his spiritual journey.

STARTING ON THE PATH OF AWAKENING

We can start our spiritual journeys at any time and, wherever we are on the path, we are influenced to one degree or another by the society we live in. From the time of birth, we learn what is expected of us to co-exist in our society. We are shaped by our families and teachers, and influenced by our peers into becoming the people they expect us to be; or those of us with a rebellious nature may become the opposite of what these influential people want us to be. Either way, the ego is molded by society's expectations. We all find places for ourselves within the shared reality that we call the mass consciousness, and, for most of us, the ego is in charge.

We develop much of the unconscious programming that creates the ego's fears, beliefs, attitudes, and judgments before the age of seven. During this time, we are highly impressionable and learn the basics of acceptable behavior in the family structure and, to a limited degree, in society. This programming establishes our values, conscience, and idiosyncrasies. It also provides us with ways to develop skills and talents that fit into the social structure.

Between the age of seven and the time of puberty, we receive most of the remainder of our programming and learn more from the society around us. From around the ages of fourteen to twenty-one, with the onset of adolescence, our orientation shifts away from our immediate family to our social group. In our teens, we are most strongly influenced by our peers. We are also acting independently for the first time, so we often make a lot of mistakes. As time passes, however, and we reach our early twenties, we begin to stabilize into our place in the mass consciousness.

Our early experiences provide us with the knowledge we need to exist in our society and a starting point on the journey of self-discovery. However, until we are able to connect with our soul and move onto our spiritual path, attempts to improve our lives are generally limited to refining the ego by replacing one program with another. People in this position may seek more money, less stress, and other ways to fill the growing voids in their lives. Ultimately, however, the emptiness they find within themselves is the absence of deeper meaning in their lives. This is where the spiritual journey begins.

Awakening is an exciting and mysterious process. We never know what awaits us around the next corner.

As we progress, we can take consolation in the knowledge that we are not alone on the journey. As mentioned previously, each of us holds a place in the divine plan for humanity, and we are being assisted by the ascended masters, angels, and guides who are reaching to us from higher dimensions of reality. You may have an awareness of your connection with these marvelous beings, and, regardless, you are receiving the help you need to keep you on the path.

Because each of us is playing a part in the divine plan, we are all exactly where we need to be on the journey. Just as it is not better to be in high school than elementary school, it is not any better to be in the sixth stage than the second stage. Wherever you are is perfect for you. The important thing is to embrace the journey, not race to completion. It is often the wounded ego that wants to compare one's position with others.

THE SEVEN SPIRITUAL ACTIVATIONS

Knowledge of the activations and their impact on your life may be your most practical tool on the spiritual path. Once you understand the sequence, you can track your development step-by-step and bring deeper meaning to the events of your life. You can also avoid the pitfalls that prevent people from progressing, and move toward a loving and joyful life.

Each activation involves learning specific lessons. If you know what the next lesson is, you can work through it more easily. Studying the activations can also help you to understand more about what the people around you are experiencing. This can enhance your relationships with others. On the spiritual journey, your body is your vehicle. Much like a car, it provides a way for you to maneuver in your reality. Before starting down the path, the ego is driving around in the traffic jam we call the mass consciousness with little or no idea of where he or she is going. Pain and fear are the ego's normal companions. From there, the stages are:

1. **Recognition:** The wounded ego sees a friendly face at the side of the road, stops, and picks up the soul. You recognize that there is more to life than meets the eye.

2. **Renunciation:** While the ego continues through the traffic, the soul begins to guide you out of the congestion. You realize that the mass consciousness has been controlling the direction of your life and begin to release yourself from its grip. It is time to move in your own direction.

3. **Empowerment:** Now you need to shift your focus on power from outside sources and understand that your power lies within. Retrieving your power brings a new sense of freedom, which continues to unfold over time. This takes you out of the traffic jam into the unknown territory of the spiritual journey.

4. **Embracing:** Your interest in the soul's journey moves to the forefront. The soul guides the ego through the unknown territory, removing any obstacles that block your way. Clearing this path helps you to embrace your true identity and connect with higher dimensions of reality. As your travels have been made easier by the efforts of those who preceded you, the path you clear now also clears a wider path for those who follow.

5. **Sovereignty:** The clearing you have done gives you a broader

perspective on life. You recognize how deeply the mass consciousness influences all of our lives and move toward the achievement of self-reliance.

6. **Integration:** With sovereignty, you now come to an understanding of how society at large is held in limitation. You prepare to drive back into the mass consciousness with the goal of helping others to steer clear of the congestion and creating a more meaningful life based on love and joy rather than pain and fear. This is when your full understanding of the nature of our reality emerges.

7. **Transcendence:** Armed with a high degree of awareness of the third dimension and the lessons we are here to learn, the soul guides you into the expression of your divine purpose and co-creation with the divine plan. Completion of this activation represents genuine freedom. It is the equivalent of living in the higher dimensions while remaining on the physical plane.

Referring back to The Continuums of Change in Figure 1.1, you can see how the relationship between the soul and the ego is transformed in the process of awakening. In *Seat of the Soul*, Gary Zukav describes the experience of transcendence, when the personality learns to fully serve the soul, as the ultimate goal of the evolutionary process and the reason for living.

As mentioned earlier, each activation is accompanied by an increase in spiritual light, unconditional love, and conscious awareness. Each stage also has a specific focus, and your perspective broadens as you come to understand our reality from increasingly higher and broader perspectives. As you move through the stages, more of your soul expresses itself in your life. Each activation also connects you with your soul in higher and higher dimensions.

There is a summary of The Seven Spiritual Activations in Figure 2.1. As you read this material, you may wonder where you are in the process. It is best to filter this question through the wisdom of your soul, because the ego is not equipped to understand it. The ego usually wants to know how it compares with others, while the soul seeks higher truth. In the next part of the book, you will have an opportunity to connect with your soul's wisdom to assist you with this and other questions.

Regardless, if you are at the point in your growth where following your soul's path is a priority, you are well on your way. You have probably gone through at least the first three stages, maybe more. Even if you are just testing the waters, you are heading in the right direction. Relative to the overall population, few people have completed all of the activations. Nonetheless, the numbers are growing exponentially, and more people are moving onto the path each day.

As a note, we address the question of how you can tell where you and others are on the journey, along with many other aspects of the process in the Clairvoyant Series described in Appendix D.

Now we will cover each stage in more detail.

FIRST ACTIVATION – RECOGNITION

Before starting the spiritual journey, we exist within the limits of the mass consciousness, largely controlled by the beliefs of the society around us. In many ways, people in this situation are unable to think for themselves. When asked for opinions, they frequently refer to an outside source for validation, such as the way their family does things, what the church dictates, what their doctor recommends, and so on. Their motivations are largely unconscious and there is no genuine spiritual connection to provide guidance. This condition is characterized by denial, including denial of how the actions of each individual relate to the whole and denial of the problems within the systems that run our society. In this regard, being a religious person and being on the spiritual path are not necessarily the same thing.

We begin the journey with the realization that there is more

FIGURE 2.1
THE SEVEN SPIRITUAL ACTIVATIONS

ACTIVATION AND FOCUS	LESSON
1. RECOGNITION Connecting with the soul	Bring first layer of physical, emotional and mental imbalances into alignment with soul.
2. RENUNCIATION Discovering our uniqueness	Release the need for approval of others to move forward on the path.
3. EMPOWERMENT Moving forward onto our own path	Develop the roots of self-empowerment, starting to find one's own expression.
4. EMBRACING Loving all parts of oneself, moving into present time	Clear personal blockages from the past, including childhood and past lives, and open fully to the energy of the soul.
5. SOVEREIGNTY Achieving self-reliance	Integrate personal archetypes, group archetypes, and most of our remaining co-dependent patterns.
6. INTEGRATION Having complete understanding	Integrate societal archetypes, overcome limitations of family history.
7. TRANSCENDENCE Reaching fruition, expressing the soul's purpose	Complete final level of clearing to express our divine purpose and co-create.

FIGURE 2.1
CONTINUED

NOTES ON EACH ACTIVATION

1. RECOGNITION: This is when we open to considering the possibility of a more meaningful reality and a deeper meaning to life. The way a person experiences this awakening depends on his or her religious and cultural background.

2. RENUNCIATION: As the deeper meaning of life sinks in, we notice how other people and groups exert control over us and free ourselves to follow our unique paths. We discover the pleasure of being ourselves, and prepare to unite with a higher aspect of the soul.

3. EMPOWERMENT: The desire to follow the soul's path and find our unique form of expression move to the forefront. This is accompanied by the birth of a new sense of freedom and personal power, as we connect with the soul at a higher level.

4. EMBRACING: With our new strength, we now uncover the blockages that have been preventing us from fully embracing ourselves and our souls. As this clearing progresses, the connection with the soul gains strength and we learn to accept ourselves and others more.

5. SOVEREIGNTY: Now we start working on an archetypal level. We focus now on clearing patterns that prevent us from fully expressing the soul's truth, creativity, and divine purpose, both personally and in our relationships.

6. INTEGRATION: When we have cleared our personal blockages and relationship patterns, we are ready to help to clear the archetypal patterns that affect our whole society and to assist humanity in moving to a higher form of expression.

7. TRANSCENDENCE: The pieces all fall into place now. We are ready to clear any remaining blockages to the soul's expression and to fully embrace our purpose. In the process, we open fully to our higher awareness and the soul's wisdom.

to life than meets the eye. We recognize that the physical body and physical existence are not all there is, that a spiritual essence exists within us. Some people move directly onto the path at birth. Others may be held up by blockages in the personality that prevent them from moving forward. These late bloomers may have to undergo a shocking experience or "hit rock bottom" to get them started.

Completing each stage requires us to clear blockages relating to the problems we encounter. In the process, we experience changes in awareness and in our energy systems. We summarize the clearing, changes in awareness, and energetic changes that occur during each stage.

Clearing in the First Stage:

- We start on the physical level by starting to bring our physical desires into alignment with the soul. Serious addictions and abuses to the body may need to be overcome to complete this stage, as we prepare the body to be a vehicle for the soul.

- Next, we start to balance our emotions, recognizing that if we want to be free, we need to control them instead of allowing them to control us.

- On the mental level, we begin to examine the beliefs and attitudes that prevent us from having true understanding.

Changes in Awareness:

- We begin to recognize how our thoughts, feelings, and physical well-being are all connected.

- As we complete the activation, our physical, emotional, and mental aspects are brought into alignment with our souls, and we begin to become aware of the spiritual path.

Energetic Changes:

- The First Activation includes an initial clearing on the physical, emotional and mental levels of the aura. This prepares the energy field to merge with the light of the soul.

- With the completion of this activation, the heart begins to open to embrace the soul.

- The aura expands and begins to build spiritual light.

Since the wounded ego is still largely in control, this stage can go by virtually unnoticed. Nonetheless, once we recognize the soul as a true force in our life, we are drawn forward by a desire to move beyond the restrictions of the mass consciousness and examine our true identity. This propels us into the Second Activation.

SECOND ACTIVATION – RENUNCIATION

This is the first of two stages that prepare us to merge with a higher aspect of the soul, the oversoul or higher self. We call it the Renunciation, because this is when we start to release the need for others' approval to move forward on the path. Most people who have experienced the Renunciation know what it means. It can be a pretty difficult time. After merging with the soul in the First Activation, everything looks different. We take a fresh look at our relationships and the organizations that have had a strong hold on us.

Up until this point, we have stayed within the nest of the mass consciousness, because it is comfortable and safe. The thought of leaving evokes fear of the unknown. We are afraid that we will lose the support of those we care about if we dare to leave the nest, if we dare to fly. Inside the nest are shared beliefs about what is right and wrong, good and bad, possible and impossible, along with what we to wear, what to eat, how to behave in public, and so on. We have all been influenced by these shared ideas, and we have learned some valuable things.

At some point, however, we must also recognize the lessons of the mass consciousness as stepping stones in our spiritual

development, rather than ends in themselves. Now we jump
out of the nest.

Clearing in the Second Stage:

- Now we release the blockages that hold us within the mass
  consciousness. Some people may experience this as a time
  when they feel they have to stand up for themselves with their
  families; they may feel a need to move beyond the limitations
  of the beliefs of their churches; or maybe their jobs lose their
  appeal and they feel a need to move on to something that is
  more fulfilling.

Changes in Awareness:

- This stage involves recognizing that we need to make our own
  decisions in life. Within the mass consciousness we have become accustomed to allowing others to run our lives for us.
  Now we need to establish our own direction. Synchronously,
  situations come up in our lives to push us forward, much as a
  young eagle is pushed out of its nest and forced to fly.

- We know more about who we are, where society ends and
  where we begin.

Energetic Changes:

- We gain even more spiritual light in preparation for connecting directly with the oversoul.

Leaving the nest does not necessarily require us to reject
our families, friends, or religions. As we will see when we explore archetypes in Chapter Nine, rebellion is simply another
expression of the ego. We can acknowledge how our cultural
heritage and traditions provide a rich framework for our lives.
Some people just need to increase their awareness of the mass
consciousness, others need to remove themselves from the relationships that create fear and limitation. These restricting relationships can prevent them from expressing their true divine

selves and experiencing more joy, love, and freedom.

As we progress on the spiritual journey, we find ourselves drawn to the places and experiences that further our awakening. The main point of leaving the nest is learning that we need to take control of our lives and follow the soul's calling. This activation is not the final step in our separation from the limitations of the mass consciousness; it is more like the kick-off point. We find ourselves going through more stages of separation from society's limitations in the later stages.

Taking Flight

We have already seen several examples of how our dreams may relate to the experience of awakening. In Appendix A, we provide more information about dreams and suggested techniques for interpreting them.

Many people on the spiritual path also have dreams about flying. Jane has had many such dreams in which she suddenly realizes that she is not limited to walking. She takes off and soars freely through the air, viewing the world from a new perspective. Then doubt creeps in. She begins to question if she really can fly and starts to descend. As long as she stays in doubt she continues falling, but when she again recognizes that she can fly if she believes she can, she soars back upward.

This dream scenario may sound familiar. The awakening of the soul opens us to new possibilities. It also forces us to question our beliefs and experience life in our own unique ways. This brings up all of the fears, and doubts that have kept us in the nest for so long: Am I really doing the right thing? Is the soul real or am I just imagining it? Should I just forget the whole thing and go back to the way things used to be?

Moving onto your soul's path is usually uncomfortable and often accompanied by rejection of those who want to keep you in the nest. Regardless, the soul's calling is generally too strong to ignore, and once you experience the freedom of flight, it is hard to go back to the old ways.

Another common metaphor that relates to this stage is the feeling of jumping off a cliff. One time in a visualization process, Jane saw herself standing on the edge of a cliff overlooking a vast sea. She felt that she had to jump off, but was afraid of facing the unknown. Understanding the symbolism, she finally leapt off the edge and plunged into the water, feeling that she was reaching into the depths of herself. The water was a beautiful deep blue and felt exhilarating as her body swam freely along. She spent a fair amount of time under the water, feeling it cleansing and energizing her.

Then Jane bobbed back up to the top and noticed a small boat nearby. She swam easily to the boat, pulled herself up over the edge, and basked for a while in the warmth of the sun. As she lay there drying off, she reflected on the experience of jumping off the cliff and decided that it had worked out okay. But she still felt uncertain about where she was going. She continued lying there, drifting aimlessly. Knowing that things are usually better than they seem, she asked herself what was the worst thing that could happen. She decided that the worst thing that could happen was that the boat would sink.

As if someone had heard her fear, the boat promptly sank. Jane found herself back in the water. Looking around again, she noticed that there was a larger boat nearby. The beautiful yacht quickly pulled up beside her. It was much better than the other boat, and it had a captain, who pulled her aboard. Together they cruised off into the sunset. She knew then that she would be fine.

This process was filled with the types of imagery that relate to the spiritual journey. There is usually a strong fear of moving into the unknown, but the positive results defy our fears and somehow surpass our expectations.

How do you feel about moving forward on your spiritual journey? Take a few deep breaths and focus for a moment on what it means to you to separate from the mass consciousness.

What changes have you made or do you need to make to be able to move firmly onto your spiritual path? And what images come to mind to describe your feelings about this? In the next chapter, we will begin to explore ways to release any fears and doubts you may be experiencing.

THIRD ACTIVATION – EMPOWERMENT

Now we reap the rewards of our efforts in the second stage. We really begin to come into our own. We move out of the safety of the mass consciousness onto the soul's path and strive for genuine empowerment. As we claim this power, we begin to experience our individuality in a whole new way. Energetically, this empowerment coincides with merging with the oversoul, provides more energetic strength and soul awareness.

As with the Second Activation, almost everybody who has completed this stage recognizes its significance. Around this time, you may find yourself searching for a new hairdo or even a whole new wardrobe as you begin to embrace your true identity. Freeing yourself from the hold of the mass consciousness allows you to express yourself in a new way that is influenced less by external forces and more by your inner guidance. We all have the need for self-expression through art, music, writing, cooking, dancing, or whatever brings us joy. We also have a need to express our soul's truth. Both of these needs begin to surface in this stage. With this comes an expanded awareness of our inner vision and inner knowing.

Clearing in the Third Stage:

- Releasing blockages that prevent us from experiencing our inner power and moving consciously onto the spiritual path.

Changes in Awareness:

- When we merge with the oversoul, we experience genuine power for the first time.

- We recognize following the spiritual path as our main focus in life. This new perspective allows us to see things much more clearly; we begin to wonder about our divine purpose and to consciously seek the soul's influence and guidance.

Energetic Changes:

- Merging with the higher self produces an energetic connection between ourselves and the multi-dimensional aspects of the soul that many people experience as a bright light above the head. Before now, this connection would have looked like a thin thread, without much substance. With this activation, it widens and becomes the conduit that allows us to receive direct guidance from the oversoul.

The first three activations relate to the physical, emotional, and mental aspects of our reality. The lessons we learn help us to release the limitations that hold our awareness in the third dimension. The fourth stage creates the bridge to higher levels of awareness we embrace in the latter stages of the journey. We learn that the bridge to the spiritual realms is made of love.

FOURTH ACTIVATION – EMBRACING

Along with the elation of recognizing that each of us is an individual with a purpose, we eventually realize that fulfilling our divine purpose involves releasing the blockages that have prevented us from recognizing our true identities in the first place. This is the purpose of the Embracing. This process started with the First Activation, but it emerges now as a conscious goal to embrace the wounded parts of ourselves and move forward on the spiritual path.

The Subpersonalities

The wounded parts of ourselves are called subpersonalities.

Together, they make up the ego. They are actually fragmented aspects of the soul who have been cut off from its light and wisdom. Instead of being one integrated whole, each of us has many separate parts with differing thoughts and feelings. We are actually a group of isolated subpersonalities who need to be reintegrated with the soul, so we can return to wholeness and awaken to our true divine selves.

One way of viewing the spiritual journey is as a process of re-integrating these subpersonalities, which include wounded parts from childhood, adulthood, and past lives. Each subpersonality experiences unresolved emotions, limiting beliefs, and judgments that need to be cleared to remove the fragmentation. As these emotions, beliefs, and judgments are cleared, we replace darkness in the aura with light and grow spiritually.

The fragmented parts synchronously show up in the areas of our lives that do not run smoothly. Take the example of an overweight person we will call Amy, who is a binge eater. Unknown to her, there is a fragmented part of her soul who is controlling her eating habits. As long as this part is in control, it is unlikely that she will be able to stop bingeing and start to lose weight. When she integrates the fragmented part with the whole, she has a real chance of reaching her desired size.

The fragmented parts come in pairs: the one we can accept consciously and the one we cannot accept consciously, who has withdrawn into the unconscious. With Amy, the part who does the bingeing is unconscious. Because of this, she may not even know why she feels the need to eat excessively. There is also another part who is conscious, who may have a perspective like "I don't care." Whenever Amy tries to address the bingeing, she encounters the part who says "I don't care." To find out what is really happening, she has to look more deeply within herself, to uncover and reintegrate the unconscious part.

Clearing in the Fourth Stage:

- Integrating the fragmented parts of ourselves that prevent us from experiencing wholeness and unity with all of life.

- Releasing our fears and moving toward a state of joy, love, and freedom.

- Healing the wounds from the past. This generally includes both inner child and past life trauma.

Changes in Awareness:

- This stage could also be called "opening to love." As we clear the unresolved emotions, we open to an infusion of light and unconditional love, so we can love ourselves and others more.

Energetic Changes:

- Upon completing this activation, we hold a new frequency that is not as easily influenced by the energy of those around us. The ego now yields to the wisdom of the soul, which helps us to feel more stable on the spiritual path.

- With the soul gaining strength, we now create a field that helps those at a lower vibration to rise to our frequency and progress on their spiritual paths. The light we radiate around us also sheds light on the darkness in others. This can make some people uncomfortable, particularly those with strongly defended personalities. They may not be able to deal with what they see in themselves when they are around us.

We will address ways to reintegrate the subpersonalities, clear blockages, and bring in more spiritual light in upcoming chapters. Addressing these patterns provides an even greater sense of power as you recognize that the subpersonalities do not have to control you, that you can bring each one back to wholeness. Ultimately, you become the master of the different parts of yourself, rather than allowing them to control you.

Many people experience the Fourth, Fifth, and Sixth Activations as a period of monumental change. This is generally accompanied by a desire to allow extra time for introspection and healing. It is a natural part of the process. As a caterpillar retires into its cocoon to make its transformation into a butterfly, we go more deeply within ourselves to complete our spiritual transformation.

After releasing another layer of blockages that have stood in the way on an individual level, our perspective again broadens, and we notice that there are patterns at play that influence groups of people and even society at large. We are ready to embrace the higher levels of our awareness in the Fifth, Sixth and Seventh Activations. This is also when the possibility of expressing the soul's divine purpose fully emerges, along with the ability to co-create.

FIFTH ACTIVATION – SOVEREIGNTY

Now we begin to work on an archetypal level. Archetypes are images, symbols, and personality types that come from the mass consciousness of a group, culture, or humanity as a whole. The term refers to characteristics of the traditions and institutions that make up our society. Our main focus here is on recognizing the archetypes as parts of ourselves that we need to understand and integrate to complete the spiritual journey. Each of these archetypes has limitations that we need to overcome and strengths that we need to integrate to move fully into living our divine purpose.

Understanding archetypes leads us more fully into our own power. Focusing on the roles we play as individuals also leads us to examine the archetypal roles we play in our relationships.

Clearing in the Fifth Stage:

- The goal now is to release the co-dependent patterns that link us energetically and psychologically to those around us. To manifest our soul's purpose, we need to move beyond limiting relationships that prevent us from being ourselves.

- Relationships that cannot overcome the bonds of co-dependence may fall away. On the other hand, relationships that are ready to move to a higher level gain strength as the individuals involved learn how to support each other in their spiritual development.

Changes in Awareness:

- The achievement of sovereignty represents the completion of the work that started in the Second Activation with the Renunciation. It provides a new sense of personal strength, accompanied by an ability to achieve one's true purpose in the face of criticism or disapproval. This is important; we cannot fulfill our divine purpose if we are unduly influenced by those who disagree with us.

Energetic Changes:

- Now we move into a state where we are largely free of energetic ties to those around us. This is what allows us to be unaffected by the disapproval of others.

- As the energy field gains strength, we become more grounded. While most people are not actually present in their bodies in the current moment, we are beginning to stabilize. In fact, at his stage, we have enough energetic integrity to assist in stabilizing the planet itself with our frequency. As we move forward, rather than becoming less worldly, we become more connected with all that is and energetically support the awakening of all of humanity.

With the completion of this activation, the focus on soul purpose gains more strength. We are clear enough now to get a clear glimpse of where we are headed.

SIXTH ACTIVATION – INTEGRATION

When our attachments to others are released, our awareness

again expands, and we become more and more cognizant of how society as a whole is functioning in fear and limitation. As we transform our fears into unconditional love, we may also feel a desire to help humanity to move to a higher level of expression. When we reach this stage, we have enough light and love to become a positive influence on a larger scale.

This stage involves tapping into the societal archetypes that underlie the mass consciousness. Here we find patterns for how the organizations and institutions function within a society. This even extends to how different cultures and countries relate to one another.

Clearing for the Sixth Activation:

- The goal now is to release the limitations within ourselves that contribute to the fears that are common to whole cultures, organizations, and institutions. If you are afraid of the police or the Internal Revenue Service, they have power over you. If you believe that you may not survive if you lose your job, your employer has power over you. To complete the lessons of the physical plane, we have to transform all of these fears and limitations into love and freedom. We have to see all parts of our society as a unified whole that can transcend the limitations of the third dimension. We will explore the societal archetypes in detail in Chapter Eleven.

- Along with these societal archetypes, we reach into the deepest levels of limitations in our family's cultural history. Here we release the patterns that have held our entire family lineage in fear. This often brings up more inner child work.

Changes in Awareness:

- With the completion of this activation, we have integrated the lessons of the physical plane. Now we have the full picture of our third dimensional reality.

- Completing this activation leaves us free to attain the ultimate goal: co-creation of our divine purpose, which is the focus of the Seventh Activation. Some are able to begin to manifest their purposes before reaching this stage. Some may have been in professions that aligned with their purposes for many years. In all cases, however, a deeper level of understanding comes with the completion of this stage.

Energetic Changes:

- The frequency of unconditional love permeates the entire aura at the end of this activation, including each of the energy centers we describe in Chapter Six.

- The energy field is largely clear and stable.

- Grounding in the body in the present moment is stabilized.

With complete understanding, this activation largely frees us from the hold of the societal archetypes. Now we can look at our lives from a higher perspective. We see that it is by rediscovering ourselves and our soul's purpose that we will find solutions to the complex problems we face individually and as a society. Albert Einstein said, "The problems that exist in the world today cannot be solved by the level of thinking that created them." We now bring a higher perspective into the mass consciousness and provide the possibility for all of humanity to shift into a new reality based on joy, love, and freedom.

SEVENTH ACTIVATION – TRANSCENDENCE

This is the time when all of the pieces come together as we complete the shift into the expression of our soul's purpose in all aspects of our life. At this level, we are approaching the right end of The Continuums of Change in Figure 1.1. With a high degree of awareness, we now focus on being responsible for ourselves and our creations. In a way, this stage is optional, in that it requires a firm commitment. It is for those who want to consciously participate in humanity's awakening.

To complete the Transcendence, we must be willing to examine all of the recesses within ourselves where remaining fear, anger, and unresolved issues are hidden and do what it takes to release them. The goal is to be able to reliably maintain a loving state in which we do not harm ourselves or others emotionally or energetically. This is important, because living our soul's purpose and co-creating with the divine plan requires us to be committed to being a positive force in all that we do.

This does not mean that we will never experience negative emotions or limiting beliefs again. Instead, it means that we can recognize imbalances quickly and release them with greater ease, so we can return reliably to the high frequency of co-creation. This is why we focus so strongly on providing clearing techniques. They allow you to be self-healing.

As the term Transcendence implies, completion of this activation also produces significant energetic changes. We do not turn into light and disappear. Instead, we bring the frequencies of the higher dimensions into this reality. Ultimately, this will allow all of humanity and the planet itself to shift into a new way of being.

Clearing for the Seventh Activation:

- Now we release most of the remaining fears, limiting beliefs, and judgments in the unconscious mind and energy system. This particularly includes releasing any limitations that relate to our abilities to co-create with the divine plan.

- Any remaining close relationships that are based on limitation usually fall away by this stage. The soul now oversees our lives and these relationships do not resonate with this energy. Close relationships must have a spiritual purpose to bring joy. The desire to be with like-minded people comes fully to the forefront now. At the same time, we feel love and compassion for all people, regardless of where they are on their journeys.

- We take full responsibility for our lives, releasing obligations that are not related to the expression of our divine purpose.

Changes in Awareness:

- Positive emotions like trust, honor, and compassion largely replace fear and limitation.

- We now have full awareness of our soul's purpose, along with the tools we need to co-create.

- Some gifted people are able to fully develop their higher senses during the earlier stages. The remainder experience an awakening of their multi-dimensional awareness in this stage. As a note, practice is required to understand the information our higher senses are transmitting. As mentioned previously, developing these senses is like learning a new language, so sensitivity and understanding improve with use.

Energetic Changes:

- When the final layer of the limitations of our third dimensional reality are released, the qualities of our higher physical, higher emotional, and higher mental awareness merge with our third dimensional awareness. Our creative expression and our physical expression become one, and the cellular fear of death that sustains life is released. From this point on, our creative force regulates our life force and desire to be alive.

- The energy field takes on a new configuration, where the light emanates from the center of one's being. The aura is completely stable and grounded.

Consider moving into a higher dimensional reality where your physical expression and your creative expression become one. Rather than being motivated by a fear of death, which is what normally sustains the body on the physical plane, you are motivated by your desire to co-create. For most of us, this is a new idea; yet it is the natural result of unifying the physical and the higher physical levels of our awareness. Emotionally, this means that our joy and vision of what we are here to create merge. Mentally, our beliefs and our inner knowing unite. Co-creation includes the ability to receive clear guidance from your soul, along with the guides and angels who are working with you from the higher dimensions.

ACTUALIZING THE GOAL OF AWAKENING

You can see that awakening is a lofty goal. As mentioned previously, many people are progressing quickly and experiencing transformational shifts in awareness. Because of this, some individuals feel a need to reduce their external activities and take more time for themselves while integrating the extraordinary changes they are experiencing. As they near the final stage, they find themselves stabilizing, and again become more active while experiencing a new perspective on life.

Fortunately, we are not in a race to the finish. Each of us moves forward at our own pace in accordance with our divine purpose. While the ego sees the spiritual journey as a competition, where the goal is to be the best and the first to the finish line, the soul understands that the journey itself is where true fulfillment lies, as we gain more understanding of ourselves and our reality.

Some people stop at specific places along the way to allow their families or those they are in direct contact with to catch up. If they are too far ahead, those around them may feel alienated. This also applies to people with public roles who need to resonate energetically with those around them. Others may stop because they are unwilling to look at the blockages that are preventing them from embracing more spiritual light.

The ego may also use degrees of perfection as a way to measure its progress. The journey is not toward perfection; in fact, aiming for perfection can hold you back. However, you do have to be aware of what your experiences are designed to teach you. Even the masters who reach down to us from the higher dimensions are still evolving and experiencing higher activations on other planes of reality.

Transcending the limitations of the third dimension is a natural process that we will all achieve sooner or later. There is no single formula, but understanding the activations can help you to stay on your path and experience the freedom of being yourself. Now, with an understanding of the soul's reality and a map for where we are going, we are ready to bring out the second key and connect directly with the soul.

CONNECTING WITH YOUR SOUL'S REALITY

CHAPTER THREE

Experiencing the Soul

*Within you there is a stillness and a sanctuary
to which you can retreat at any time
and be yourself.*

–HERMAN HESSE

We all have access to a wealth of information about the soul, but reading about it is not the same as experiencing its presence. When a student or client asks us what direction they should pursue, we sometimes ask what his or her soul's guidance suggests. This is the most practical place to look. Unfortunately, with little direct experience to draw on, most people are unable to answer. And, without a direct soul connection, many enter into a state of confusion and despair as they venture onto the spiritual path. They know that the old ways are no longer working, but lack access to the soul's wisdom to guide them forward.

Fortunately, this confusion is unnecessary. Accessing the soul's guidance is a skill that anyone can develop.

OPENING TO THE SOUL

We already know that connecting with the soul's reality transcends the limitations of the five normal senses. At the same time, even a moment's contact with the soul is more memorable than most of our day-to-day experiences. Some people have had near death experiences, which they overwhelmingly understand as proof of the soul's existence beyond the confines of the physical body. Many more people have seemingly timeless moments when the beauty and connectedness of everything becomes clear. At these times, the fears, limited thinking, and judgments that normally hold them down are replaced by feelings of tremendous joy, an outpouring of love, and a sense of the unlimited possibilities our lives offer.

These soulful moments usually happen by chance, but may be stimulated by exposure to sublime works of art, music, fine food, or the beauty of nature. The mere thought of standing on a mountaintop, surrounded by a vibrant blue sky and billowy clouds, looking over the vastness of our magnificent earth, can change our concepts of reality.

Each person's experience of the soul is unique and memorable.

A walk in a beautiful natural environment may stimulate a person's soul. Another person may respond more deeply to exquisite strains of music or inspirational lines of poetry. And from our experience, most people can experience the soul by turning their focus to their inner world with a guided visualization process that we call Soul Centering. Creating this connection is the focus of this chapter.

If you are new to relaxation and visualization techniques, we want you to understand how easy it is to go from your normal state of awareness into a relaxed state, where you can open to your inner world and the realms of the soul. You start by relaxing the body. This is also a way to relax your mind and open to what is below the surface of your awareness, much like focused daydreaming. It is easiest to achieve this kind of a relaxed state when you are in a quiet place.

We will start with an example that you can use to achieve a mild state of relaxation to feel more centered and good about yourself any time. Of course, you should not use relaxation techniques while you are driving or involved in activities that require your undivided attention.

Here are some tips to help you improve your success with guided visualizations.

- **Allow plenty of time.** The hectic pace of life is not conducive to self-discovery. You need to set aside plenty of time for exploration of your inner world. Part of the ego's control is based on keeping your life moving at such a rapid pace that you do not have time to look within. Exploring the realms of the unconscious and the soul cannot be rushed. You need to make the time you need to look within yourself a priority.

- **Create a relaxing environment.** As you begin to explore your inner world, you will learn how nurturing and enlightening it can be. To receive the most from a guided visualization, you will want to create a positive setting where you can open to this expanded state of awareness. This space is just for you, with no outside distractions. To enhance the experience, you may want to play soft music and/or light a candle in the room. You may also want to cover yourself with a cozy comforter or blanket if you tend to get cold.

- **Set the rational mind aside.** As you begin the visualization process, set aside your rational mind and logical thinking. This may take a bit of practice, because, for most people, the rational mind is accustomed to providing a play-by-play analysis of everything that happens. Learning to set it aside is a major key to your success. You want to go into a quiet place within yourself where your multi-dimensional awareness can become active. One suggestion is to tell your rational mind that you want it to wait and evaluate the experience later, when you are done. This generally calms the chatter and frees you to experience what is happening in the visualization.

- **Open to your higher senses.** As your mind relaxes, shift your focus to your body and your five senses. A guided visualization is not limited to seeing. Notice how your body feels and the sounds you hear around you, along with what you see with your closed eyes. You will also want to open to your higher senses: your inner sight, feeling, and hearing. Some people even experience smells and tastes as a part of their visualizations. Each person is unique in this area; some feel more, some see more. Rather than expecting anything specific to happen, just allow the experience to reveal itself and be what it is. Your higher senses can open you to a new way of experiencing your life and yourself. Including as many of your senses as possible will allow you to move more deeply into the process and experience it in a more real way.

- **Allow the process to unfold naturally.** As you open to your inner world, the unconscious mind often expresses itself with imagery and symbolism. You will receive the best results if you just accept whatever you experience without questioning it, even if you do not understand it at first. The rational mind may want to come in and negate the experience. But everything you see has meaning, so it is best to simply allow the process to unfold in an organic way. With practice, the experience will reveal wonderful, magical things, and the meanings of the symbolic images will generally become clear as a natural part of the process.

Those who are familiar with guided visualizations have probably experienced them in group settings or through the use of an audio tape. The processes in this book are designed for you to read. Just take your time and pronounce each word slowly to yourself as you follow the directions. Whenever you wish, you can close your eyes to focus on the visualization and explore the process more deeply.

THE VALUE OF JOURNALING

We have already begun to see that we are moving into more subtle forms of awareness as we reach to the soul. Such experiences, and the results of clearing on these levels, are often rejected by the ego, which wants to keep us in the familiar range of the five physical senses.

Dr. Roger Callahan, one of the forerunners of the meridian-based techniques that led to the development of EFT, called this phenomenon of denying change the "apex problem." His solution was to have his clients measure the intensity of their issues on a scale of one to ten (where ten is the greatest possible intensity) before starting to make changes. Those who use EFT are familiar with this practice and understand the benefits. It adds focus and a way for the rational mind to measure the changes that occur during the healing work.

Throughout this book, you will notice suggestions to focus on how you feel both before and after a process, and to write these feelings down. We recommend having a notebook and journaling your experiences as you open to the profound reality of your soul. This will increase your awareness of the changes you are undergoing and help you to integrate your experiences. You will reap the rewards of your efforts. And what you perceive as small shifts in the moment often become major changes over time.

Although journaling is one of your most valuable tools for maintaining your focus and integrating your experiences on the spiritual path, many people resist doing it. This is because writing is so concrete. When you put something down on paper, you cannot ignore it. The ego may not want to commit itself in this way, but we all have to learn to overcome the resistance of the ego to move forward.

Fortunately, you can use the tools in this book to overcome any resistance you encounter. EFT is very effective and, if you are not familiar with it, this would be a good time to start. Refer to Appendix C for instructions on using the EFT Short Sequence. You will be glad you did, if it helps with your journaling. Statistics show that people who write down their goals are much more likely to achieve them. Similarly, writing down your experiences helps you to integrate them and reach new levels of understanding.

Here are some reasons for journaling:

- **Staying focused:** If your mind wanders during a visualization process, keeping a running commentary of your experience can help you to stay on track.

- **Recording the details of your journey:** When you reach new levels of understanding while in a relaxed state of awareness, it is easy to forget the profound realizations you have had. At one time or another, we all experience life-changing revelations in dreams or moments of clarity. When this happens, we think that the understanding is so profound and important that we could not possibly forget it. But we often do, and, later, when we try to remember, the profound revelation is gone. Writing provides a record for future reference.

- **Validating your multi-dimensional experiences:** Remember the apex problem. Those with strong rational minds have a tendency to minimize the importance of experiences they have while in deeper states of awareness, or to negate them altogether. Writing provides a way to recreate the power of the experience. Kathleen Adams, Director of the Center for Journal Therapy in Lakewood, Colorado, and author of *The Way of the Journal*, says, "Writing gives voice to the innate wisdom that resides within each of us."

- **Improving your mental and physical well-being:** Research has shown that writing can actually improve some of the physical symptoms of diseases such as asthma and arthritis. For traumatic experiences, James W. Pennebaker, author of *Opening Up*, says that "what writing does is help the individual come to terms with that event. And, eventually, that reduces the stress."

- **Accessing unconscious feelings:** Writing is a powerful tool for bypassing the conscious mind. When painful emotions come up, just start writing freely, "letting it all come out" on paper. You can also write down the realizations you come to while you are connected with your soul. This provides a way to monitor your progress as you move to higher and higher levels of awareness.

- **Integrating your experiences:** Writing is a valuable tool for understanding an experience. Even if you never read what you have written, the act of writing engrains the experience deeply into your awareness and helps you to integrate it more easily.

The practice of journaling can become a positive force in a person's life. One such person considers her journal to be her best friend. Through this medium, she is developing a profound relationship with her soul.

THE POWER OF THE BREATH

Most of us take our breathing for granted and pay little or no attention to it. We are unknowingly ignoring one of our most powerful resources. In addition to bringing air into the lungs, the breath moves energy around in the body. Of course, most people do not take full advantage of the breath. It certainly does not help that society teaches us to keep our stomachs tucked in. This even prevents us from completely filling our lungs with the oxygen we need to sustain life, not to mention moving energy through the body.

With awareness, you can learn to use the breath as a transformational tool. Some qualities of the breath:

- **Physically,** the breath sends oxygen into the lungs. From there it is transmitted to nurture all of the cells of the body.

- **Energetically,** it sends energy through the body and the surrounding energy field, nurturing and nourishing your entire being. You can use your awareness to move energy around and energize your body. You can also become more aware of your natural use of the breath. A deep sigh or yawn often accompanies the release of stuck energy. If you notice yourself unconsciously taking a deep breath, you can bring awareness to what has shifted. You can also consciously take a deep breath to release stuck energy.

- **Emotionally,** it may be used to focus your awareness on a specific part of the body or to painful emotions, to release the energetic blockages that are causing the pain.

- **Mentally,** it may be used to shift your awareness from the ongoing dialogue in your head to the sensations in your body. Then, by breathing slowly and deeply, you can quickly alter your state and achieve feelings of relaxation and well-being.

THE BREATHING PROCESS

For those who are new to these techniques, this first process shows how easily you can change your state of awareness by focusing on your breath. Before starting, take a moment to note how you feel physically, emotionally, and mentally. When you are ready to start, just focus on reading each word slowly to yourself in a relaxed way and following the directions.

Begin by shifting your focus from your mind to your body. Notice how your body feels and notice how your breath feels as you inhale and exhale. In a moment, we will ask you to stop reading, close your eyes, and take a few deep breaths. As you do this, imagine that you are taking in pure, fresh air, and fill your lungs completely so your stomach moves out freely, like a baby's.

Then as you exhale, imagine that you are releasing all of the tension in your body, and exhale completely. Take your time, and enjoy each breath fully. Close your eyes for a moment, and focus on enjoying a few deep breaths now.

Amazingly enough, most people notice a marked difference in their state of awareness just by taking a few deep breaths. A lot of the tension we experience comes from shallow breathing, so you can easily change your frame of mind by focusing on your breath and allowing yourself to relax. This also increases your body awareness and helps you to feel more present.

Next, take a few more deep breaths and, as you inhale, do it in a loving way, nourishing and nurturing yourself with each breath, feeling the loving energy flowing throughout your body. Close your eyes for a moment and take a few deep, loving breaths.

You should feel noticeably different by now. This is a wonderful way to take a break and feel good about yourself. As you continue reading, focus again on your breath and imagine sending pure, loving energy throughout your body, to release tightness in your neck, shoulders and back, to relax eye strain, to release tension anywhere in your body. Allow the energy to flow all the way down your arms and legs to the tips of your fingers and toes. Take a moment now to close your eyes and focus on sending this loving energy throughout your body.

If you have thoughts running through your head, you can also clear your mind with your breath. Imagine that you are sending pure, clear energy into your brain, allowing the thoughts to simply drift away. Notice how your mind feels clearer with each breath, until all of the unnecessary thoughts are gone.

Make note of how you feel now compared with how you felt before you started the Breathing Process. You may want to go through this process a few times, until you can complete it without the script. It is so simple, you can use it almost anywhere to reduce stress and increase your ability to focus. And it doesn't take any extra time to take a loving breath. It is just a choice you can make any time you think of it.

While doing this process, some people may notice a place in the body that they can not love or where the body holds tension. We will be exploring this more, but you can begin to understand that the areas that are tense, painful, or unloved usually correspond to blockages that you need to release to embrace your soul's presence.

THE SOUL CENTERING PROCESS

Now we are going to build on the Breathing Process with the Soul Centering Process, which allows you to consciously focus your awareness on your soul. This process helps you to move into the state we mentioned earlier where your soul overrides the dominance of the ego. For some, this may be a new experience that strengthens over time.

Before proceeding further, place this book in one hand and point to yourself with the other hand. Notice where your hand is pointing. Interestingly, even though most of us identify ourselves with the thoughts that go through our minds, when asked to point to ourselves, we usually point to our hearts. And when we want to emphasize something, we use a phrase like "I believe (or feel) this with all of my heart." It is uncommon for a person to say that he believes something with all of his head. And in a moment of deep feeling, a person may place his or her hand on the heart, as if focusing on the energy there.

At a deep level, we all recognize
the significance of the heart.

The soul's expression comes most strongly through the heart and through feelings of love toward ourselves and others. The heart forms the bridge between our limited reality and the higher reality we are connecting with on the spiritual journey. Paul Pearsall, Ph.D., a psychoneuroimmunologist who works with heart transplant patients, describes its profound importance in his book *The Heart's Code.*

We can learn to decipher the heart's code by silencing the brain, quieting ourselves, focusing on our heart, and sensing what it has to say and what memories it may bring forth from the cells that store it. The heart has its own form of wisdom, different from that of the rational brain but every bit as important to our living, loving, working and healing.

Doing the Soul Centering Process and focusing on the feelings in your heart is a way to open to the expression of your soul. When used over time, this process allows you to develop an ongoing relationship with your soul.

Whether you are new to spirituality or have been exploring it for many years, you can benefit from this process. It helps you to develop a loving relationship with the magnificent person you truly are, and to connect more and more deeply with the joy of being yourself. Like the Breathing Process, with practice, you can achieve this state quickly, in any place and any time. This helps to strengthen your soul's presence, so that it can regain its rightful relationship to the personality and provide input on all aspects of your life.

Before you start, write down how you are feeling. This will allow you to compare your current state with the way you feel when you have completed the process. Make note of how your body feels physically, how you feel emotionally, what kinds of thoughts are going through your mind, and how you feel about yourself. If there are any problems that are bothering you, make a note of them, too.

Now you are ready to start. Like the Breathing Process, the Soul Centering Process is designed for you to read. You can allow yourself to relax, focusing on saying each word slowly to yourself. Then close your eyes to visualize when instructed or whenever you want to deepen your experience. In a quiet, comfortable place, you should be able to maintain your relaxed state and focus as you alternate between reading and closing your eyes to visualize.

Begin as you did with the Breathing Process. Take a few deep, loving breaths, imagining that you are inhaling pure light and energy and, as you exhale, that you are releasing all of the tension from your body, so that with each breath, you feel lighter and more relaxed. Allow this wonderful feeling to reach every cell of your body, as you become more and more relaxed. Close your eyes for a moment now, and take a few of these breaths.

Now feel yourself relaxing even more, so that with each breath, you feel more peaceful, and your body becomes even lighter, allowing any tension you notice to drift down your body, arms, legs and feet, into the earth. Notice that even as you continue reading, you can go into a pleasant state of relaxation, guided by your breath.

Now focus on taking more pure, loving breaths, bringing clear energy into your mind with each inhale, so all of the cells of your brain can relax, and any thoughts from the day can simply drift away. Notice how your mind becomes clearer with each breath. And, as you continue to read, allow the clear energy to drift downward so that your entire head relaxes, including your forehead, your jaw and mouth. Feel the relaxation traveling down your neck and shoulders now, again allowing any tension in these areas to melt away, so that your neck and shoulders feel completely relaxed.

Now allow a wave of clear energy and relaxation to move gently down your arms, past the elbows and wrists, all the way to the tips of your fingers. Feel another wave of relaxation moving down from your shoulders so your torso can relax, and all of the organs in your body can relax, drifting down your chest, relaxing the lungs and heart, the stomach and down past the waist, allowing all of the organs in your abdomen to relax. Now feel the relaxation moving down your spine, so your back can relax, melting further into your seat. And allow the relaxation to move down your thighs, to the knees, the ankles, and the feet, all the way to the tips of your toes, so your entire body is relaxed and filled with clear, light energy.

As you continue to read, focus your breath on the area around your heart, which is where your soul is most firmly connected with your body. Imagine that you are sending pure light into this area, so each breath brings in more energy. And as you continue breathing, feel the energy building so there is a ball of light around your heart, and this light becomes brighter and brighter, radiating its energy out in all directions. Pause for a moment now, and feel your soul's energy radiating out around you.

Now feel yourself completely surrounded by the energy of your soul. Feel it permeate every cell of your body with its beautiful light. As you do this, if any pain comes up in your heart, simply allow it to come fully into your awareness, because releasing this pain will help you to completely embrace the love you hold in your heart. If necessary, you can close your eyes and continue to breathe pure energy into your heart to allow any pain you are experiencing to release.

Now shift your focus to the area above your head and imagine that there is another light there. This light is your higher self or oversoul, which is your connection with your soul in the higher realms. Close your eyes for a moment now if you want to visualize the light more clearly.

As you imagine it there, allow this higher frequency of light to pour down through the top of your head and fill your entire body, so you can see and feel yourself filled with the light all the way down to the tips of your fingers and toes. As it becomes brighter and brighter, allow it to overflow so that you are completely surrounded with this light and you can feel yourself in perfect harmony and balance with everything around you. Close your eyes for a moment, and see and feel this light from your higher self.

Now, as you continue to breathe, imagine that each breath contains even lighter air. Notice that you feel so light that you can imagine yourself gently rising up off the ground and drifting gently toward the sky. As you travel along, you will find a peaceful place where you can relax, maybe on a mountaintop or a billowy cloud. Close your eyes and allow yourself to drift to this elevated place. When you arrive, just relax there for a moment, and notice how it feels to be so light and how the energy of your soul feels to your body and your emotions. If you were feeling any conflict before you started this process, notice if it has changed. Close your eyes, and allow all of your senses to experience your soul's energy and the peaceful scene around you.

As you become accustomed to being in this soulful state, you can use this opportunity to bring your soul's perspective to any questions or challenges you are dealing with. Take a moment to do this now, if you wish.

As a note, if you were not able to fully experience your soul's energy, you can continue to use this process and you will notice a shift as you become more aware of the different frequencies of energy. Make particular note of any troubling emotions you are experiencing and what they remind you of in your life. Simply experiencing these emotions, breathing pure energy into them and allowing them to release will bring you closer to experiencing your soul. As a note, you may also want to use EFT or Spiritual Kinesiology to release these troubling emotions, once you have learned these techniques.

Now, shift your awareness back to the present time and feel yourself where you are, making note of your body's position. And, as you breathe, allow your breath to bring you back to your normal waking state, feeling alert and alive, bringing your higher awareness with you into your daily life. You may feel like moving around a little, wiggling your toes and fingers, and stretching a bit. As you continue to feel the light of your soul glowing in your heart, count from one to five, feeling more alert and wonderful with each number: one, two, three, feeling more awake now, four, and five, feeling completely awake and filled with love.

Now review what you wrote about how you felt when you started the process and compare it with the way you feel now. Notice how you feel physically and emotionally, what kinds of thoughts are going through your mind, and how you feel about yourself. Write down any changes you notice.

Exploring your soul is like any learning process. At first, you may feel awkward and unsure of yourself, just like learning to drive a car. And like driving, your skills and confidence improve with practice. Exploring the realms of the soul has the added challenge of being unverifiable by normal means. You cannot go to the Department of Motor Vehicles, take a test and come out with a license for accessing your higher self. But we will explore ways that you can validate the power your soul can have in your life with kinesiology.

We have used the Soul Centering Process personally for many years and still find ourselves growing from the experience as more truths are revealed to us. We also use it regularly with our clients and students to help them to connect with their true selves. Here are some of their descriptions of the experience of being centered in the soul:

- "It's a stillness, stopping activity and busyness; a quiet, centered place, not for or against, neutral without controlling."

- "I experience an expansive unconditionally loving energy that transforms conflicts."

- "A bright, sparkly, energetic feeling comes over my whole being, a knowingness and expansive feeling."

- "I feel totally open, with a large expanse above me. It is very uplifting, connecting to my higher power. There is so much more than I ever realized."

- "Warmth flows like a river from my head through my body."

- "Being centered in my soul creates a serene and peaceful view of life. Everything is as it is meant to be."

- "It is an absolute knowing that all is well. I am at peace with myself in the world."

- "I feel deep peace and tranquility. With that comes a heightened sense of knowingness free of fear, negativity, and uncertainty. I'm a different person, the person I am meant to be, with all of the fragmented aspects blended into one."

- "It's realizing that the small plane I've been having so much trouble flying has actually been on auto pilot, and is in reality the Starship Enterprise. Not only do I have intergalactic access and multidimensional capabilities, but there's an on-board computer system that tells me anything I need to know. And all is joy and all is love. Of course, this only happens for a few minutes at a time, but it's enough to let me know that it's my natural state."

There is a common sense of peace, acceptance, and expansiveness in these experiences. You may also notice that the messages from your soul become clearer as you progress on the spiritual journey. In the early stages, fear can interfere with the divine truth that your soul wants to share. It is much like the effect a storm has on radio transmission. As the storm subsides, the transmission becomes clearer. Similarly, your soul's transmissions become clearer as you attain higher levels of truth and connect with your soul more deeply.

Now we will add to our exploration of the deeper levels of our awareness as we explore the profound nature of symbolic imagery.

CHAPTER FOUR
Imagery as the Language of the Soul

Close your eyes and you will see clearly.
Cease to listen and you will hear truth.
Be silent and your heart will sing.
Seek no contacts and you will find union.

–LAO TSU

Discovering the unimaginable depth and beauty within yourself is one of the most precious rewards of the spiritual journey. Exploring the higher realms is like opening an ancient treasure chest filled with priceless jewels and examining them one by one.

Without the proper perspective, however, many people are put off by what their first glimpses reveal. The jewels may look dirty or dusty after spending countless years in the chest without care. Similarly, the jewels within ourselves have been tarnished by the blockages that mask our inner beauty. Any painful sensations, emotions, beliefs, and images we experience are significant aspects of our inner worlds. These disturbances can actually alert us to the discoveries that await us. Beneath them lie the priceless jewels.

Using imagery is one of the best ways to experience the power and beauty of the soul.

The images we sense with our inner vision are often symbols that reveal truths about our reality and ourselves in ways that words alone could not express. Their significance may not be immediately apparent, and it may not be necessary to interpret every image that comes along. Nonetheless, your experiences can be greatly enhanced by focusing on the images you see in your exploration of your soul and while doing the visualization processes in this book.

We will also discuss how you can incorporate the use of symbols to explore different aspects of your self. Introducing symbolism intentionally opens the communication lines with the unconscious and with the soul.

THE POWER OF VISUALIZATION

Many people believe that they cannot visualize. This is not accurate. Some have expectations of what it should be like. When their experiences do not match these expectations, they reject them or stop themselves from allowing the images to unfold in a natural way.

As a person with an active rational mind, this was a challenge for Jane. She would ask her unconscious mind to communicate directly, if there was something she needed to know. Over time, she realized that this is not how the unconscious mind works. Symbolic imagery is its primary means of communication and it is beyond the range of the rational mind. Interpreting the imagery triggers a more profound level of understanding that reaches deep within one's being.

Here are more common reasons why people block imagery:

- Some people were criticized as children for having wild imaginations or for saying they saw things that were not considered normal. Children sometimes perceive things that adults are unaware of, like angels and fairies. Their parents may be afraid of this type of violation of the limitations of the five senses, and belittle their children for mentioning their perceptions. Over time, these children frequently limit their perceptions to exclude anything that might cause ridicule.

- Although visualization is beyond its realm, the rational mind may set up rules for what it should be like. Some people expect that they should see the images in cinematographic color with surround sound, just like in the theater, and anything less is not worth considering. This is another way the ego works to undermine the experiences of the soul. These individuals may block their experiences, because they do not live up to their expectations. The images they see in their visualizations may be subtle or more like an inner knowing. This is how it is for both of us. We do not see images like a photograph, but know what they are and can describe them in detail. In fact, it is often by describing the images that we recognize them. Journaling can also help with this.

- Many people doubt the correctness of the images they perceive. This is why it is so important to allow a visualization to unfold in its own way. When an image surfaces, you probably will not understand its meaning immediately. Sometimes, the rational mind steps in, feels foolish, and tries to make it go away. It is important to stay with the image. If you start a guided visualization process and see the image of a hand holding a candle, what do you do? Just stay in the flow of the experience and accept the image.

  If necessary, you can ask your rational mind to withhold its judgment until later, after you have completed the process. You do not need to know what the image means right away. The hand with the candle may be leading you to a mysterious place where you will find some of the jewels you have lost. Or the candle may expand and turn into a bright light that surrounds the world. You will never find out what it means unless you stay with it and allow its significance to unfold.

It is easy to confirm your ability to visualize. Imagine that you are reading a little book to a child at bedtime. The cover reads *The Alphabet,* and on each page there is a letter and an image representing a word that begins with that letter. You open the book and start with the first page. On it you see the letter "A" and a picture. Close your eyes for a few seconds and imagine the page. Now ask yourself, what does the picture on the page with the letter "A" represent? If anything comes to your mind, such as an apple or an airplane, then you have successfully visualized it. Now you will have a chance to practice on something more meaningful.

THE HEART FOCUS

The Heart Focus is a short and profound visualization process that can help you to hone your skills and connect with your heart. We recommend familiarizing yourself with the Soul Centering Process before attempting this one.

This process also includes the optional use of EFT to clear any issues that come into your awareness. Clearing these blockages can help to strengthen your soul connection. If you are unfamiliar with EFT, refer to Appendix C for instructions on the EFT Short Sequence. This simple technique is effective most of the time. Also, have your journal handy, so you can record your perceptions during the visualization.

Start as you have before by shifting your focus from your mind to your body. Feel yourself resting in your chair, and notice how wonderful your breath feels as you inhale and exhale. Take a few deep, deep breaths, allowing yourself to relax more with each one. Imagine that you are inhaling pure, fresh air, filling your lungs completely. Then as you exhale, just allow any tension in your body to begin to melt and drift gently down into the earth below you. Take your time and fully enjoy each breath. Close your eyes for a moment and focus on enjoying a few deep breaths.

If you have thoughts running through your head, take a moment now to clear them with your breath simply by sending pure, clear energy into your mind and allowing the thoughts to drift off into the air. Notice how your mind feels clearer with each breath, until it becomes completely relaxed.

As you continue reading, focus your attention on your heart. Imagine that you can visualize your heart like a valentine and notice how it looks. Write down your observations about each of the following questions. Remember that even if you do not see a clear image in your mind, you probably still know what it looks like. Or imagine what it would look like if you could see it.

> *What is the color of your heart?*
> *How does it feel physically?*
> *How does it feel emotionally?*
> *What is its shape?*
> *How do the edges look?*
> *Are there any cracks, holes or other features in it?*
> *When it beats, how does it sound?*
> *Is there anything else about it that you need to be aware of?*

Looking at your heart in this way may bring awareness to an issue you need to address and positive qualities you possess. You may also have perceptions that you do not understand. Remember that you can probably bring more awareness and healing by connecting with your soul, if you wish to follow up in this way.

When you have finished writing down the details of your visualization, start to direct your breath to the area around your heart again, focusing on the energy of your soul. Imagine that you are sending pure energy into this area, so with each breath there is more and more energy in your heart. And as you continue breathing, you can feel the energy building until it seems that there is a ball of light there around your heart, and this ball of light becomes brighter and brighter, radiating its energy out in all directions. Pause for a moment now, and continue breathing energy into this area.

Now feel yourself completely surrounded by your soul's energy. Let it permeate every cell of your body with its beautiful light.

Now shift your focus to the area just above your head and imagine the light there. Allow this light from your higher self to pour down through the top of your head and fill your entire body, so you can see and feel yourself filled with the light all the way down to the tips of your fingers and the tips of your toes. As it becomes increasingly brighter, allow it to overflow so that you are completely surrounded with this light and you can feel yourself in perfect harmony and balance with everything that is around you. Close your eyes for a moment, and see and feel the light from this higher aspect of your soul.

From this point of connectedness with your soul, go through what you wrote down about the image you had of your heart and allow your soul to tell you what each perception means. For example, if the color was not clear, ask yourself why. If the shape was not uniform and symmetrical, ask why. If there were cracks, holes, or other features, ask what each one represents.

If you cannot bring the meanings into your awareness, ask again, and write down the responses as you receive them. This may help you to bypass the rational mind. And to finish, ask your soul if it has a special message for you about your heart. Again, the message may come out most clearly if you just start writing it. Take as much time as you need now to review the images.

If the answers you sought did not present themselves, trust that they will come in their proper time, as you integrate the experience. Meanwhile, if any unresolved emotions came up in your visualization, you can use EFT now for clearing, if you wish. When you are done, return to the visualization, and notice if the image has changed. As a blockage releases, the image changes, too. You may learn more by reviewing the image again.

When you are finished, shift your awareness back to the present time and feel yourself where you are, making note of your body's position. And, as you breathe, allow your breath to bring in active energy to help you to return to your normal waking state, feeling alert and wonderful. You may also feel like moving around a little, wiggling your toes and fingers, and stretching a bit. Counting from one to five, you will feel more and more alert: one, two, feeling more awake, three, four, and five, feeling completely awake and loving yourself.

This visualization is a powerful example of how you can use symbolism to stimulate awareness. As the place where the soul centers in the body, the heart is a powerful image, with layers of significance. There may have been more symbolism that was revealed than you could interpret in a single sitting. If that was the case, you may want to return to it over time and explore it more. As you progress with this book, more of the heart's significance may be revealed to you through time.

In addition to being a powerful process to use by yourself, the Heart Focus is a wonderful technique to use with others. It provides a way to find out what is blocking the soul's expression, so it is a good starting point for any soul-oriented work. This process is also good for ongoing use, because it will continue to reveal more as you move forward on the spiritual path.

The images people discover in the Heart Focus represent both the blockages they need to clear and the expansiveness they have achieved. Some people experience a combination of both. Here are some examples of painful heart images our clients have experienced with this process:

- The heart is throbbing or beating nervously or irregularly.

- There is a sword through the heart.

- A sword was removed from the heart a long while ago, but the heart is still bleeding uncontrollably.

- The heart is dark and heavy.

- The heart is dirty.

- The heart is burning at the edges.

- The heart is hidden behind a door, stored away in a closet drawer.

- The heart is filled with holes, like pencil points punctured through it.

- The heart is hurting.

- The heart is working too hard.

- The heart is off kilter, skewed, or unbalanced.

As mentioned previously, when such blockages are cleared, the image of the heart changes, too. The dark and heavy heart lightens; the burning heart cools; the overworked heart relaxes. After you have progressed further in this book, you can also use Spiritual Kinesiology to clear any blockages you encounter in the Heart Focus.

Fortunately, there are also wonderful rewards for the efforts we make on the spiritual journey. The Heart Focus may produce beautiful images of expansiveness that help us understand how far we have progressed. Here are some positive images our clients have experienced.

- The heart is a beautiful shade of pink with soft, rounded edges.

- The shape of the heart is full and nicely rounded.

- A dove of peace sits in the center of the heart.

- The heart looks like a light without edges that radiates brightly in all directions.

- The heart beats melodically, like beautiful music.

- The heart feels warm, open, and inviting. It is filled with love.

- The heart looks and smells like a brilliant, red rose.

- The heart is a calm, emerald lotus, with soft, open petals.

These inspiring examples show how the heart is opening and embracing the soul.

HEALING IMAGERY

In this book, we will explore symbolic imagery connected with some challenging situations in your life. This imagery is created by the soul to illustrate something, so that you can change and grow.

One time, Jane was working with a client named Judith. When Judith focused on her problem, she saw the image of a barren landscape with dead grass and a gray sky. The wind was blowing, sounding like a moan. Judith felt depressed. This was not a place she had been. Rather, her unconscious mind was expressing how dismal life was for her at that time. As she and Jane continued and brought more of Judith's soul awareness to the situation, the barren landscape gradually transformed itself into a beautiful green forest with tall trees, a blue sky, puffy clouds and a bright golden sun overhead. Birds were chirping and she felt wonderful.

Even those who do not know much about imagery can probably understand the differences between the initial image and the final outcome. When you are shown dismal or painful images, your soul has a solution to the problem and wants to reveal it to you. The visualization processes we explore in this book are designed to facilitate this transformation. You just need to be open-minded and willing to follow the processes. Opening to the unconscious mind and the soul is a creative and enlightening experience. Every cloud has a silver lining.

Of course, not all images you see in a visualization process are symbolic. Some may simply be who or what they are, and this becomes apparent as you progress in your explorations. Often, there is a combination of literal and symbolic meaning woven through the imagery.

With the understanding that you are being shown symbolic images to help you to learn and grow, it follows that it should be possible to find out what they mean. It may take some practice, but, while in a soul-centered state, we usually just ask ourselves, "What does this mean?" The key is to be open to the response.

Fortunately, there is no need to stay with difficult imagery for long. Spiritual Kinesiology generally transforms it in a matter of minutes, so this is what we will explore next.

CHAPTER FIVE

Using Spiritual Kinesiology

Whatever you can do, or dream you can, begin it.
Boldness has genius, power and magic in it.

–GOETHE

With a soul connection and an understanding of how the mind works, you are ready to begin to make some changes. When you thought about moving into a life filled with joy, love, and freedom, did you experience any doubt, fear, anger, or other unresolved emotions? If so, these imbalances may prevent you from moving forward on your spiritual path.

This chapter provides tools that you can use to transcend the unresolved emotions, limiting beliefs, and judgments that we all encounter on the spiritual path. Kinesiology can detect the energetic blockages that you are ready to release as you progress with the activations. It can locate imbalances that are completely unconscious and answer questions about your soul's development. Muscle testing provides a way to validate your soul's experiences and can serve as the first step in developing your intuition. The addition of your soul's awareness and the powerful Spiritual Kinesiology healing techniques provide an easy way to clear the imbalances you find.

As mentioned previously, one of the benefits of these techniques is that they are non-invasive. The recipient does not have to know the source of a problem or relive a traumatic experience for SK to be effective. Of course, this defies the common belief that progress has to be slow and painful, but aligns with our approach to awakening. We need to understand ourselves to move forward, but we do not need to dwell on our difficulties. The goal is to transcend them easily, so that we can experience more joy, love, and freedom.

Here is how Carl Carpenter, the originator of Hypno-Kinesiology, the forerunner of SK, describes the beauty of this approach in his *Hypno-Kinesiology for Professionals* manual:

> With the Hypno-Kinesiology program we find and release the source trauma simply and without the individual having to relive the experience. Once this emotional load is released, the individual senses an inner growth and maturity. Over a period of weeks subtle changes take place, and within a few months there is renewed strength, emotional and physical, and a new person emerges. This has a two-fold benefit: the changes are coming from within naturally, and the changes are coming at a rate of speed that they will handle easily. Their mind will not allow them to be harmed by making dramatic changes too quickly.

Another note for those who are wary of hypnotherapy: the receiver of SK is awake and aware during the entire process. In fact, most people find it pleasant and enlightening.

SPIRITUAL KINESIOLOGY STEP-BY-STEP

This chapter covers the basic SK techniques. You will find a variety of ways to use them in the chapters that follow. First, you need to be familiar with kinesiology (muscle testing). We described how to do muscle testing in the EFT book. For those who are unfamiliar with it, we have provided an edited excerpt from that book in Appendix B to teach you how to do muscle testing with one or two people.

You can use SK with another person or by yourself. We will describe using the techniques with two people, the provider and the receiver, with notes on how you can make adjustments to do them alone. All of the SK techniques are based on six easy-to-learn steps. Once you know them, you can use any of the processes in this book. These are the steps:

1. **Preparation:** Help the provider and receiver to achieve a centered and neutral state of awareness.

2. **Muscle Testing:** Perform testing with kinesiology to locate or confirm the existence of imbalances in the energy system.

3. **Setup:** Identify the specific issue you want to address.

4. **Evaluation:** Measure the intensity of the issue.

5. **Balancing:** Provide balancing using your soul's energy with two hypnotherapy techniques: reframing and anchoring.

6. **Re-Evaluation:** Re-evaluate the intensity of the issue.

Now we will describe each step in detail.

STEP 1: PREPARATION

Preparation focuses on eliminating anything that might interfere with the accuracy of the muscle testing. The environment and any people involved need to be neutral, so the provider and receiver are both open to receiving information through kinesiology. Before starting any testing with kinesiology:

1. The provider should be in a neutral state, feeling centered and grounded. To further enhance the experience, the provider can connect with his or her soul with Soul Centering.

2. Be sure the environment is neutral, with no distracting music, scents, and so on.

3. Prepare the person receiving SK. We suggest two parts to this process:

   • First, have the receiver drink some water, if available. This brings oxygen to the brain and optimizes brain functioning, which is necessary for obtaining accurate results.

   • Second, do a brief centering process to place the receiver in a neutral and receptive state to receive information through muscle testing. The script in Appendix B is a suggested starting point. You may also want to use the Soul Centering Process when this would be appropriate for the receiver.

STEP 2: MUSCLE TESTING

When you start the SK process, you may have an issue in mind that you want to address; you may want to understand a problem more fully; or you may just feel out of balance, without knowing why. This is where the muscle testing comes in. We provide SK checklists through the remainder of this book that you can use to locate imbalances or understand more about any kind of difficulty you may experience. These versatile checklists include statements or questions to muscle test to find out what is happening below the surface of your awareness. For example, when you say, "focus on your job" or "focus on money," it brings that energetic pattern to the surface. The muscle response indicates whether the energetic pattern is balanced or unbalanced.

We recommend making copies of the SK checklists to use with the muscle testing. These questions and statements identify imbalances that need to be corrected to move forward on the spiritual path. You may also want to experiment with using your own test questions and statements. When you do, it is important to use concise wording and to have a clear understanding of what the muscle response indicates. John Diamond discusses the importance of precision in his book *Life Energy*:

> It is absolutely essential that the statement you make to test be very precise. Do not make the statements too long, and make them very exact. If the statement is long and rambling you will not be able to zero in on the thought and visualize it as clearly as possible in your mind, to focus on the test image.

Test Responses

One of the most common problems our students have with kinesiology is determining what a test response means. A balanced response is one where a statement is true or correct or where there are no blockages present. Interestingly, this does not always correspond with a strong muscle. An unbalanced response indicates the presence of a blockage. This does not always correspond with a weak muscle. We provide guidelines for interpreting responses along with the descriptions of the checklists. Here are some general pointers.

- When focusing on a time in your life, like when you were five years old, the balanced response is strong. A weak response generally pinpoints a difficult or traumatic experience that is creating a blockage.

- When focusing on a statement that requires a yes-no or true-false reaction, yes and true are strong, no and false are weak. If you muscle-test a person for a question that requires a yes-no reaction, like "Is your name Rhonda?" a strong response means yes, while a weak response means no. Similarly, if you test the statement "I enjoy my job," which requires a true-false response, a strong response indicates that this is true and a weak response indicates that this is false.

- When thinking about something that is negative or unhealthy, the balanced response is weak. When an individual tests strong in these instances, something in his or her mind understands this as a useful thing. For instance, if a woman tests strong when she thinks about being 40 pounds overweight, her mind considers the extra weight to be a positive thing. It may provide a buffer between her and those around her that makes her feel safe and secure.

- When focusing on how a negative emotion or quality affects the energy system, the unbalanced response is strong. In some cases, it may be difficult to distinguish this response from response described in the last item. You can resolve this potential inconsistency by using a yes-no question instead of a statement in such cases. If you have a problem with anger, asking "Are you free of anger?" will produce a weak response both in the mind and energy field.

- When thinking of a positive emotion or quality, like peace or love, the balanced response is strong. If you think about love and receive a weak response, this indicates that there is a blockage you need to release to bring more love into your life. In this case, focusing on how the positive emotion or quality affects the energy system produces the same response. When the positive quality is present, the response is strong. When it is absent, the response is weak.

- Focusing on an activity, event, place, or thing is tricky. A weak response probably indicates that the person being tested has a blockage. It may also indicate that there is something toxic in that environment that is negative for the individual. For instance, if a man tests weak when focusing on the office where he works, he may have a problem at work or he may be reacting to something toxic in the building. On another level, going there may not further his soul's purpose. In such cases, you may need to be more specific about what you are testing for.

- When focusing on a part of your body, the balanced response is strong. If you get a weak response to a statement like "focus on your skin" or "focus on the sound of your voice," there may be a blockage that needs to be addressed. We need to love all of the parts of ourselves. Otherwise, we are inviting injury, illness, or disease. You may also have to consider the possible presence of energy toxins, which we discuss later in this chapter. If you are ingesting something that is unhealthy for a specific part of the body, this could create a weak response. As with the previous item, in such a case, you may have to be more specific about what you are testing for.

- When focusing on another person, the balanced response is strong. A weak response generally indicates that there is a blockage you need to release to achieve sovereignty. No one should weaken your energetic system. If they do, you need to free yourself by clearing the blockage. As a note, in a small minority of cases, an energy toxin could be causing the problem. For instance, if the receiver is allergic to the perfume the person wears, the weak response could relate to the allergy rather than the person he or she is focusing on.

The key with muscle-test responses is to take your time, so you feel certain that you understand what the response to a question means before proceeding further. When testing another person, you should also expect some surprised reactions. The receiver may think that you are pushing harder with some statements than others, rather than understanding that the test muscle has gone weak. You need to use consistent pressure, but will also find that this is a common reaction regardless of how consistent you are.

The receiver may also think that he or she was not paying attention when you pushed on the arm. Saying "resist" just before you push usually eliminates this possibility, but you can always repeat the test to confirm the result. A statement that triggers an imbalance throws the receiver out of the present moment. This may feel the same as not paying attention, but it will continue to occur each time you test the statement.

STEP 3: SETUP

Once you have completed the muscle testing, you generally have to pinpoint precisely what you want to address before you do the SK balancing. With SK, as with EFT, the results are better and more likely to be lasting when you are specific. For instance, if a person has an unbalanced response to experiencing anger, the clearing will be more effective if the receiver can focus on a single time when she was angry.

This step corresponds to the EFT Setup. In *Getting Thru to Your Emotions with EFT*, we describe how there are different aspects to many issues, just as there are many trees in a forest. Clearing occurs one aspect at a time, so you may have to repeat the process to completely eliminate an issue. Fortunately, each round of clearing also weakens any remaining aspects, so after one to five rounds of SK balancing, most blockages disappear completely.

Muscle testing may also uncover more than one imbalance. In this case, you need to decide on a single item to clear. You may know what you need to address first. If not, you can pick the strongest emotion, use muscle testing to determine where to start, or just start anywhere. Interestingly, clearing one of a group of imbalances on a checklist may also balance some or all of the others.

STEP 4: EVALUATION

The purpose of this step, which directly corresponds to the Evaluation in EFT, is to measure the intensity of the issue you want to address. Whether you are doing balancing on yourself or another person, it can be beneficial to focus on the issue before and after to make a mental note of the changes that occur. Measuring the intensity of a problem has become a standard way of evaluating a therapeutic experience. You quantify the intensity of the emotion you are clearing between one and ten, where one is just a hint of intensity and ten is the greatest possible intensity. In therapeutic settings, this number is known as the Subjective Unit of disturbance Scale or SUDS.

As previously mentioned, one of the benefits of using SK is that it is not necessary to know the source of a problem to clear it. If there is no emotional intensity or physical sensation to measure, you can skip this step. On the other hand, if you can quantify it, you will have a way to evaluate your progress when you finish balancing.

The goal is to measure the effect the emotion or issue is having on you now, not the way it was in the past or the way you imagine it could be in the future. Sometimes just focusing on it brings on stress, anger, or another emotion. If not, focusing on a time when you experienced it before generally brings back the old feelings.

STEP 5: BALANCING

Now you are ready for the magic. Balancing with SK includes the use of two powerful hypnotherapy techniques: anchoring and reframing.

Anchoring

Anchoring is a term derived from NLP that refers to how a memory in one the senses stimulates a response in one or more of the other senses. Hearing an old song brings back wonderful memories. Or maybe it's the smell of a particular perfume or the color of a special dress that recreates that special feeling. These are examples of naturally occurring anchors.

Such examples seem positive enough, but some naturally occurring anchors may generate lifelong fears or phobias. A girl who was traumatized by a dog may feel the same trauma every time she sees a dog throughout her life. Or a man who received a severe spanking whenever he showed emotion as a boy may be unable to express his feelings as an adult.

Addictive behaviors are anchors in themselves. After a hard day, some people turn to a stiff drink, which they associate with relaxation. People who become nervous in social situations may smoke cigarettes to relieve their discomfort. Of course, the addictive substance enhances the result, but the behavior itself is also a powerful anchor.

We have many anchors that help us to get along in our environments. Red and green traffic lights stimulate drivers to stop and start at the right times. The sound of the school bell reminds students that it is time to go to class. Anchors provide a way for the unconscious mind to sort and retrieve information. Unfortunately, if we are not aware of them, they may be using us more than we are using them. With awareness, however, we can replace unproductive anchors with positive resource anchors. This can help us to function better, enjoy life more, and achieve our goals.

To strengthen our relationship with our soul, we can anchor in the soul's wisdom and bring ourselves more into alignment with our divine purpose.

The intentional use of anchoring was developed with Neurolinguistic Programming (NLP), an offshoot of hypnotherapy. One of its developers, Richard Bandler, defines it in this way: "Anchoring is a deliberately designed process of inserting a stimulus that will evoke a consistent response from a person."

To accomplish this response, we first need to understand how anchors are created:

- **The recipient's internal state is the key.** In everyday life, we have no control of the anchors we unconsciously install in ourselves. This, of course, is the problem. Fortunately, with SK, we can consciously anchor a positive soul-aligned state.

- **Timing is critical.** Anchors occur naturally during a heightened experience. This tells us that when setting anchors, we want to install them at the height of an experience.

- **Repetition strengthens an anchor.** If you repeat the experience you want to create, you can strengthen the anchor.

There are many ways to anchor, such as with sound, color, imagery, and touch. Here we will anchor by touching two different places on the body. Interestingly enough, on an energetic level, it doesn't matter where you anchor. We use specific locations simply for convenience.

Reframing

Reframing is another powerful NLP technique that clears blockages by replacing an unbalanced pattern with a balanced one. *Getting Thru to Your Emotions with EFT* includes a reframing process that replaces a painful image with a positive one. With Hypno-Kinesiology, Carl Carpenter reframes the negative pattern by having the receiver focus on a positive experience. You will learn how to do this here. We will also go a step further by reframing with the soul's energy and wisdom. With this technique, you can anchor your soul's wisdom into all aspects of your life and further your goal of awakening.

You will find different forms of reframing in all of the GTT processes in this book. Each process changes an unbalanced pattern in your unconscious mind and energy field to a balanced one. The most effective way to do this is to view the issue from the perspective of your soul's wisdom.

Reframing may be the single most important technique to understand as you move forward on the spiritual path. With the wisdom of your soul, you will know that the change you make is in alignment with your divine purpose, which is important, because your soul may have different goals than your ego. A common mistake people make is simply substituting one of their ego's goals with another. Unfortunately, this does not further the goal of spiritual awakening.

Take the example of a woman who is having a hard time passing the realtor's exam. By contacting her soul's wisdom, she may discover that it is actually her father who wants her to be a realtor. Her ego is complying to keep peace in the family, but her soul's joy actually wants to pursue a career in the culinary arts. This is why there is a blockage to passing the real estate exam. Her soul is trying to steer her in another direction, but she has not gotten the message. On the spiritual path, the goal is to integrate the soul's perspective on any issue.

Amazingly, an issue may reframe itself by just bringing it into one's awareness. We have seen this occur many times with our clients and ourselves. A client focusing on a painful image may watch it turn into light and feel immediately better. When an issue clears itself in this way, you may not even need to understand the entire problem. The important thing is to bring the issue out of the darkness and into the light.

Of course, it is not usually this simple, in which case the power of reframing comes in handy. As with any visualization, reframing is most effective when you involve as many of your senses as possible. This is why we focus on how an issue looks, sounds, feels physically and emotionally, and where it is located in the body. The more fully you can experience it with your physical and higher senses, the more effective the change will be. With the SK balancing techniques, the reframing can occur in just a few minutes.

The Balancing Techniques

1. **The Reframing and Anchoring Technique (R&A)** shifts an unbalanced energy pattern to a balanced one. Figure 5.1 illustrates the hand positions. Here is the process:

   A. The provider can stand or sit next to the receiver. For the purpose of this example, imagine that the provider is sitting to the right of the receiver. As the receiver focuses on the unbalanced pattern, the provider lightly places his or her left hand on the right shoulder of the receiver to anchor the pattern. After silently counting to 10, the provider releases the hand. If you are doing this process alone, place your left hand on your left knee or another place on your body.

B. Now it is time to reframe. You have two choices:

1) **Recall a Positive Experience:** This is the approach Carl Carpenter uses with Hypno-Kinesiology. The provider instructs the receiver by saying something like: "Think of a happy time in your life, a time when you felt strong and confident."

2) **Anchor the Soul's Energy:** The provider says something like: "Imagine the light above your head and allow the perfect energy to come down from your higher self to balance _____ (describe the pattern you are working on). Feel the energy coming down, surrounding you with it's healing light. When you feel yourself completely surrounded by this balanced energy, say okay."

Before using this technique, we recommend using the Soul Centering Process in Step One for the initial centering to confirm the receiver's ability and willingness to center in the soul's energy. Some people may not be comfortable with this approach; they may prefer to focus on a positive experience. As you will see in some of the examples in this book, even a person with a strong soul connection may not be able to access with the soul's energy when facing an intense issue. There is no need for concern when this happens. Just do a round or two focusing on a positive experience or start with the Finger Rolling Technique described below. Then, as the intensity lessens, the receiver will probably be able to re-establish the soul connection for the final clearing and balancing.

**FIGURE 5.1
HAND POSITIONS FOR
REFRAMING AND ANCHORING**

← A. Anchor the original
   unbalanced pattern on the
   shoulder.

B. Reframe the unbalanced
   pattern either with a
   positive experience or the
   soul's light and wisdom.

C. Anchor the balanced →
   pattern on the upper arm.

← D. Shift from the unbalanced
   pattern to the balanced
   pattern by collapsing the
   original anchor.

C. While the receiver continues to focus on the balanced pattern, the provider places his or her right hand on the receiver's right arm above the elbow to anchor it and says something like: "Continue to focus on this energy and feel it becoming even stronger." After silently counting to ten, the provider releases the hand. If you are doing this process alone, place your right hand on your right knee or another place on your body.

D. The provider asks the receiver to think about nothing and again places his or her hands on both anchors. In our example, the left hand goes on the right shoulder and the right hand goes on the right arm above the elbow. The provider counts silently to ten, then removes the hand from the shoulder. This releases the negative anchor. He or she then counts to five while leaving the right hand on the arm to reinforce the positive anchor, then releases the other hand. If you are doing this process alone, place your hands on your knees or wherever you put them before.

2. **The Finger Rolling Technique** diffuses negative energy. You can use this technique to release any degree of emotional intensity. It is helpful when there is a high level of emotion, to allow the intensity to begin to release before using the Reframing and Anchoring Technique. You can also use it to release the final remains of a disturbance, when it is down around a one or two. For those who are familiar with EFT, this serves the same purpose as the Floor-to-Ceiling Eye Roll and works equally well.

A. As the receiver focuses on and, if appropriate, talks about the unbalanced pattern, the provider lightly rolls the fingers of his or her hand along the upper or lower arm of the receiver. We do this by rolling our fingers back and forth as if we are playing a piano from the low notes to the high notes and back, over and over. This brings the pattern to the surface and allows it to release as the provider touches the same points over and over.

B. While the provider continues with the finger rolling, the receiver focuses on the problem and, if appropriate, talks about it more, as the negative energy diffuses.

C. As the final traces of the negative energy release, the provider can instruct the receiver to bring in his or her soul's energy by saying something like: "Imagine the light above your head and allow the perfect energy to come down from your higher self to balance _____ (describe the pattern you are working on). Feel it coming down and releasing the old energy."

D. As the receiver imagines the new energy coming down, the provider continues to roll his or her fingers along the arm, saying something like, "Take your time releasing the old energy. When you feel the process is complete, say 'okay'."

STEP 6: RE-EVALUATION

When you have finished balancing, have the receiver take a deep breath to allow the energy to reconfigure. The receiver may feel the energy shift over a period of a seconds or minutes. Then there are a few different ways to re-evaluate the changes.

• Have the receiver focus on the issue in the same way he or she did initially. Measure the intensity again between one and ten, and notice any changes. In most cases, there is a substantial change or the issue is completely gone.

• Retest the pattern with kinesiology. If you were not able to measure the intensity, or if the intensity is gone, muscle test to verify that the energetic imbalance has shifted.

• Discuss how the receiver feels about the issue now. The balancing process often brings unconscious information into the individual's awareness. Discussing it can lead to profound recognition of the change that occurred. While it is not necessary for the receiver to share this experience, this can help to integrate the changes. We generally offer the possibility of sharing.

If you determine that you are finished using SK, simply wipe off the anchor points with a few gentle sweeps of your hand, like you are removing dust, to complete the process. If you determine that more work needs to be done, you can perform another round of balancing.

REPEATING THE SK PROCESS

If there is any remaining emotional intensity after completing the process, or if the muscle test still produces an unbalanced response, you can repeat it. Although one round of balancing sometimes releases the blockage, several rounds are often required to bring the intensity of the issue all the way down to zero. As mentioned earlier, this simply means that there are different aspects of the imbalance to release. With each round, ask the receiver if the emotion has changed, such as from fear to anger, and continue with whatever emotion has surfaced. When the intensity is around a two or less, the Finger Rolling Technique is an easy way to release the last traces of an imbalance. For EFT users, the Floor-to-Ceiling Eye Roll described in *Getting Thru to Your Emotions with EFT* is an alternative.

The energetic shifts you make with Spiritual Kinesiology are integrated over a period of days, weeks, or even months. The receiver's innate wisdom determines the timing; it also knows how much clearing and balancing the receiver can do in a single session. Each time you start a new topic, you may want to muscle test to find out if it is okay to proceed further. Remarkably, the entire SK process can take just a few minutes. With a little practice, it is easy to do and amazingly effective. As one client commented, "It is deceptively simple, but profoundly effective in obtaining real shifts with lasting results."

Of course, there may be times when you do not receive the desired results. If, after several rounds of the process you do not seem to be making progress, there is probably something the receiver needs to understand consciously for the pattern to clear. When this is the case, try one of the GTT processes that are described in upcoming chapters in this book. We recommend the Illumination Process or the Integration Process. Including these techniques should bring your success rate close to 100 percent.

Here is an example of how easy Spiritual Kinesiology can be. Jane worked with a client we will call Brenda. When she arrived for her session, Brenda was angry with herself for being late, so they started by working with the anger. Brenda told Jane that being on time was very important to her. She was critical of people who were late, so she felt especially bad about being late herself. Testing Brenda's anger with kinesiology confirmed that she was unbalanced.

When they started the SK process, Brenda's anger measured six on a scale of one to ten. Jane performed the Reframing and Anchoring Technique, anchoring Brenda's anger on her shoulder and her soul's awareness on her upper arm. After a single application, the anger was completely gone and Brenda understood that it was unnecessary. This little process took only a few minutes and probably helped Brenda to be less judgmental toward herself and others. It also cleared the way for the deeper work that followed.

DEALING WITH ENERGY TOXINS

There is another factor that could interfere with the balancing process: energy toxins. This term commonly refers to energies and substances that irritate the energy system, which includes substances that are ingested or in contact with the body, as well as negative energies in the environment.

Interference of energy toxins is rare. Nonetheless, if you are not getting positive results with SK, an energy toxin may be the culprit. Here are some examples: foods and beverages, herbs, medications, nicotine, cosmetics, shampoos or other personal care products, perfumes, odors, discordant energies from computers, high concentrations of electrical energy, and negative people. We have particularly found energy toxins to be a factor when the receiver lives or works in a negative or hostile environment. One of our students, John, was a factory worker who was berated each day at this job because of his interest in spirituality. The other workers were clearly threatened by John's sensitivity and distinctness. Being in this type of disharmonious environment is extremely demanding on the aura. Energetically, it is like being in a war zone, where one is struggling just to stay alive. Doing any further clearing may be impossible. As a result, John was not able to make any progress with clearing his issues until he left this job.

The same is true for people who are in negatively charged relationships. The continual presence of destructive energy may block their progress on the spiritual path.

In his *Hypno-Kinesiology for Professionals* manual, Carl Carpenter describes how changes occur in each individual's own time with Hypno-Kinesiology. Sometimes the changes are immediate and profound. Sometimes they are gradual. With some issues, they do not occur at all. This is how he explains it:

> Some of these issues are protective measures provided by the mind to make life bearable, and some will stay in place until environmental changes are made. If the recipient is living in a harmful environment, change won't take place until they make a move.

It is our experience that the synchronicity of the universe supports us in moving into alignment. When a person has the strength to leave a negative situation, he or she usually finds the new environment better than expected.

To help deal with energy toxins, *Getting Thru to Your Emotions with EFT* provides procedures to follow and a list of potentially harmful influences that you can test with kinesiology. The goal is to minimize your exposure to negative energies, so you can focus your attention on your spiritual journey.

GETTING STARTED WITH SK

It is easiest to start using SK with an imbalance that you are aware of, so you can measure its intensity, and evaluate the difference in your feelings before and after the process.

Here is an example from one of our clients. Edith was experiencing feelings of frustration and powerlessness about with all the things she needed to learn to use her new computer. She summarized these feelings as being out-of-control, which she rated at an intensity of ten on a scale of one to ten. Along with this out-of-control feeling, she felt panic. After one round of Reframing and Anchoring (R&A), the out-of-control feeling was down to six. She also noticed that she felt less panicky. After just one more round of R&A, her feelings of being out-of-control and panic were gone completely. Edith knew that if she ran into a problem now, she could deal with it.

Focusing on her computer again, however, Edith now felt impatience, which she rated at an intensity of eight. As is often the case, she wanted to be able to do everything right away. After just two more rounds of R&A, the impatience was gone, too, and Edith felt that she could trust that everything would work out fine.

To get started, you can also experiment with the Basic Checklist in Figure 5.2. It includes some common imbalances, including negative emotions, activities, events, places, things and aspects of oneself. A balanced response to all of the questions and statements in Parts One, Two, and Three is strong. A balanced response to the statements in Part Four is weak. This checklist should provide helpful insight for most people. When you have finished completing the muscle tests, pick an imbalance that you can measure and complete the SK process.

Here is an example from one of Phillip's clients. On the Basic Checklist, Carla tested weak for fear. She associated this feeling with herself as a young child living with a violent mother. Her mother abused her, her father, and her sisters. Carla was afraid of the unknown and afraid of becoming like her mother. Her fear started at nine on a scale of one to ten. It was accompanied by sadness that her mother had died before Carla could get close to her. The sadness started at ten. After just one round of R&A, both were almost completely gone. In their place, she felt joy, lightness, and a sense of release from her throat. She said her heart was red and glowing, too.

Rapid transformations are common with these techniques.

Spiritual Kinesiology taps our most powerful healing source: the light and wisdom of the soul.

Another client named Betsy tested weak for the statements "focus on your weight" and "focus on exercising," which she saw as connected. She could lose weight, but would quickly regain it, attributing the problem to lack of commitment to exercise. She was too occupied with caring for others, which left little time to take care of herself. Focusing on her concerns about getting regular exercise brought an emotional intensity of six. After two rounds of R&A, the intensity was down to zero. Betsy then reflected on the importance of having time to exercise. Her preoccupation with caring for others would have to take a step back. She now felt more confident about exercising, which was unusual for her.

As often happens, this short process brought further understanding. Betsy also realized that she had not wanted to commit to an exercise program out of fear that others would criticize her for neglecting them. Now she knew that she could take care of herself without worrying about what they would say, which she could not control anyway. Having improved health would also allow her to take care of others better.

This entire process only took about five minutes. Reaching this level of awareness and understanding would undoubtedly take much longer using more traditional techniques.

FIGURE 5.2
BASIC CHECKLIST

Part 1: Negative Emotions and Qualities

STATEMENT	STRONG	WEAK
"Are you free of anger?"	_____	_____
"Are you free of fear?"	_____	_____
"Are you free of guilt?"	_____	_____
"Are you free of frustration?"	_____	_____
"Are you free of stress?"	_____	_____
"Are you free of depression?"	_____	_____
"Are you free of anxiety?"	_____	_____
"Are you free of sadness?"	_____	_____

If you experience any other negative emotions, test them.

	STRONG	WEAK
"Are you free of _____?"	_____	_____

Part 2: Activities, Events, Places and Things

STATEMENT	STRONG	WEAK
"Focus on your job."	_____	_____
"Focus on your home."	_____	_____
"Focus on your office."	_____	_____
"Focus on your next birthday."	_____	_____
"Focus on money."	_____	_____
"Focus on going to the dentist."	_____	_____

Think of any other activities, places or things that may be having a negative effect on you and test them.

	STRONG	WEAK
"Focus on _____."	_____	_____

FIGURE 5.2
CONTINUED

Part 3: Your Self

STATEMENT	STRONG	WEAK
"Focus on your heart."	_____	_____
"Focus on your body."	_____	_____
"Focus on your mind."	_____	_____
"Focus on your weight."	_____	_____
"Focus on your sexuality."	_____	_____
"Focus on exercising."	_____	_____
"Focus on the sound of your voice."	_____	_____
"Focus on being your age."	_____	_____
"Focus on being healthy."	_____	_____

Think of any other aspects of yourself that may be having a negative effect on you and test them.

	STRONG	WEAK
"Focus on _____."	_____	_____

Part 4: An Imbalance

STATEMENT	STRONG	WEAK
"Think about smoking a cigarette."	_____	_____
"Think about weighing 300 pounds."	_____	_____
"Think about being a couch potato."	_____	_____
"Think about being ill."	_____	_____

Think of any other imbalances that may be having a negative effect on you and test them.

	STRONG	WEAK
"Think about _____."	_____	_____

FIGURE 5.3
WHEN TO USE THE CHECKLISTS

CHAPTER	CHECKLIST	STAGE
5	Basic Checklist	Any
6	Current Lesson	Any
8	Subpersonalities	Primarily 1st - 4th Activations, some in 5th – 7th
9	Personal Archetypes	Primarily 5th Activation, some in 6th and 7th
9	Polarities	Any
10	Group Archetypes	Primarily 5th Activation
11	Societal Archetypes	Primarily 6th Activation
11	Family Heritage	Primarily 6th Activation
12	Transcendence	Primarily 7th Activation

A GUIDE TO THE CHECKLISTS AND PROCESSES

Figure 5.3 lists the SK Checklists in this book and shows which stage or stages in your spiritual development each one relates most directly to. You can use this list to muscle test which checklist to use at any given time with the question "Do you (or I) need to use the _____ checklist now?"

We hope you are beginning to see how useful kinesiology can be. Muscle testing is also a good first step in developing your intuitive abilities. With repeated use, many people begin to experience a knowing of the response before pushing on the test muscle. As mentioned earlier, you can also ask yes or no questions on any subject imaginable.

CHAPTER SIX
Getting Thru Energetically

We live each day with special gifts that are a part of our very being, and life is a process of discovering and developing these God-given gifts within each one of us.

–JEANNE DIXON

Exploring the realms of the soul includes a study of the energy that runs through us, around us, and unites us all. The human energy field or aura holds specific information about the soul and our divine purpose. Blockages in the energy field point to what is preventing us from unlocking the soul's gifts.

According to quantum physics, we are energetic beings living in a sea of life force energy. This energy nourishes us as much as the air we breathe, the food we eat, and the water we drink. It flows around us and through us and sustains life. As it enters the aura, life force flows through the energy system to the physical body, nourishing all of the organs and cells.

The aura is composed of layers or levels containing different frequencies of energy that gradually step down in vibration from the higher dimensions where the oversoul exists to the physical body. In this book, we explore the seven levels that surround and interpenetrate the body. These layers define our entire reality. From the physical level, each level extending outward holds a higher frequency, or more subtle form of energy. Many people can feel these subtle vibrations with their hands and clairvoyants can see them with their inner vision.

Barbara Ann Brennan describes these levels in her illuminating book *Light Emerging*:

> These levels, or energy bodies as many people call them, cannot be considered less real than our physical body. If all of your energy bodies are strong, charged, and healthy, you will have a full life in all areas of human experience. If your energy field is weak at any level, you will have difficulty having experiences that are associated with that level, and your life experience will be limited. The more levels or bodies that you have developed, the fuller and broader your life experience will be.

Opening to your soul and your divine purpose includes exploring all of these levels and strengthening each one.

THE SEVEN ENERGY CENTERS

Corresponding to the seven auric layers, there are seven energy centers, or chakras, each of which extends from the body through all seven levels. These centers collect higher frequencies of energy, and step them down through the layers to nourish the aura and the body. Figure 6.1 illustrates The Seven Energy Centers. Along with the seven major chakras, there are hundreds of minor chakras all around the body.

The major chakras look roughly like funnels of energy that are located between the base of the spine and the top of the head. The first one, at the base of the spine, points downward. The next five are like double funnels pointing out the front and back of the body below the navel, in the area of the solar

FIGURE 6.1
THE SEVEN ENERGY CENTERS

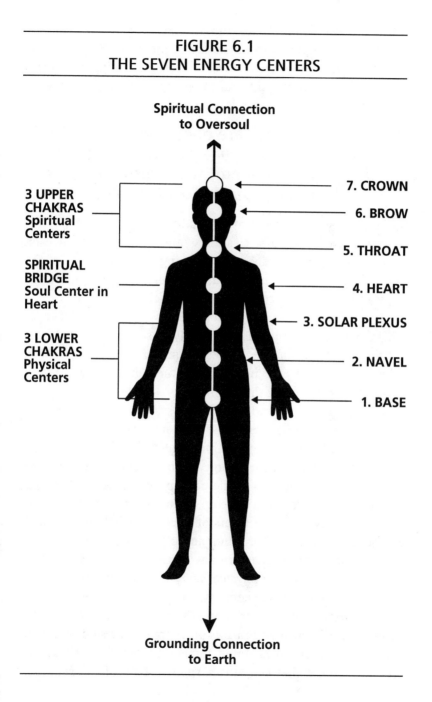

Spiritual Connection
to Oversoul

3 UPPER
CHAKRAS
Spiritual
Centers

7. CROWN

6. BROW

5. THROAT

SPIRITUAL
BRIDGE
Soul Center in
Heart

4. HEART

3. SOLAR PLEXUS

3 LOWER
CHAKRAS
Physical
Centers

2. NAVEL

1. BASE

Grounding Connection
to Earth

plexus, at the heart, at the throat, and at the brow. The last funnel points upward from the top of the head. Each of these centers relates to specific systems of the body, the corresponding body functions, and to specific aspects of our lives. In addition, each resonates with a specific color.

When the chakras are open and functioning properly, they connect us with higher frequencies of energy, our higher senses, and our multi-dimensional awareness.

As we awaken, the centers gradually open like beautiful flowers, providing more awareness and light. It is as if each center has a series of doorways opening into each layer of the aura. As we progress, more of these doors open, and more energy and light flow through the energy field.

In the areas of the body where we have energetic blockages or imbalances, the chakras are usually closed or out of balance, cutting us off from the higher frequencies of energy. Also, where there is disease in the body, there is a corresponding blockage in the flow of this vital energy.

The energy field and the chakra system together provide complete information about one's physical, emotional, mental, and spiritual state-of-being. Understanding the relationships between the layers of the energy field, the energy centers, the mind, and the functions of the body provides a complete picture of who we are. Each system is actually a mirror of the others, so a blockage in the layers of the energy field is mirrored in the chakra system, the mind, and often even in the body itself. Clearing the blockage in any system likewise clears it in all of the systems. The physical body is an exception, because it is just one part of the energy system.

Information about our strengths, weaknesses, and soul's purpose are all held within this amazing energy system, much the way information is stored in a computer. Each chakra is like a database that contains a specific type of information.

The following is a general description of each of the major energy centers, with the corresponding relationships to the body and aspects of life.

As a holistic map of our reality, these seven centers alternate between active and passive, or masculine and feminine energies. They may also be divided into groups that define the different aspects of our reality. The three lower centers correspond to the different aspects of our physical reality. The fourth or heart center is a bridge between our physical reality and our spiritual reality. In *Light Emerging*, Barbara Brennan poetically describes it as "a bridge between heaven and earth." The three upper centers correspond to the different aspects of our spiritual reality.

The First or Base Center

- Location: Base of the spine

- Color: Red

- Corresponding Glands and Systems of the Body: Adrenal glands, urinary tract and bones

- Lesson: Fear of physical survival and discomfort, often leading to an experience of lack or greed

- Gift: Using one's sensitivity toward the physical body and the earth to benefit the planet and humanity, viewing the body as the vehicle for the soul's expression

The base center relates to our physical existence, including our physical survival, our stability in the world, and our sense of security. Its energy is active and masculine. When it is balanced and energized, we experience feelings of physical well-being and vitality. When it is out of balance, we become concerned about survival issues and feel insecure. Imbalance also triggers the adrenals' fight or flight mechanism, which may, in extreme cases, lead to violence.

The base chakra roughly corresponds to the first or etheric layer of the aura. This layer is the energetic blueprint from which the physical body is formed. Physical problems correspond to distortions in the etheric level, which generally extends about one to two inches from the body.

The Second or Navel Center

- Location: Just below the navel

- Color: Orange

- Corresponding Parts of the Body: The ovaries or testes and the reproductive system

- Lesson: Fear of sexuality and emotions, often becoming overly sexual and/or emotional, or frigid and/or withdrawn

- Gift: Expressing joy and sexuality appropriately, nurturing oneself and others; in this state, all negative emotions have been transformed into love

The navel chakra relates to our emotions and sexuality. It is a passive, feminine chakra. In a real way it is the source of life itself. When it is balanced, we experience the joy of being alive, feeling nurtured, comfortable, and emotionally stable. This joyful state also extends to our sexuality and ability to experience sexual pleasure.

When this energy center is out of balance, negative emotions interfere with our ability to experience joy. This is where we hold painful emotions related to our childhood and our past. These emotions can leave us feeling unsupported, and, as a result, we may not be able to nurture ourselves or the people we care about. When this chakra is out of balance, our healthy sense of our sexuality and our ability to experience sexual pleasure may also be impaired.

The navel chakra corresponds to the second, emotional layer of the aura. This is the layer aura readers are usually referring to when they see all of the colors of the rainbow. It generally extends about 12 to 18 inches from the body.

The Third or Solar Plexus Center

- Location: Below the rib cage, above the waist

- Color: Yellow

- Corresponding Parts of the Body: The pancreas, the digestive system, and the muscles

- Lesson: Fear of having power in the world, leading either to misuse of or relinquishing of power

- Gift: Using true internal power and leadership abilities for the good of all concerned, acknowledging the power of others equally with one's own

The solar plexus chakra reflects our mental state and our sense of power. It is an active, masculine center. This is where we hold our beliefs and attitudes about what is and is not possible in the external world. When it is balanced, our beliefs and attitudes reflect an understanding that we have unlimited possibilities and genuine power. When it is out of balance, our thoughts are controlled by limiting beliefs and attitudes that prevent us from reaching our soul's true desires.

The third center roughly corresponds to the third or mental layer of the aura. This layer looks like a radiant yellow sun that extends about two to three feet from the body.

The Fourth or Heart Center

- Location: In the center of the chest, around the heart

- Color: Pink or green

- Corresponding Parts of the Body: The thymus gland and the circulatory system

- Lesson: Fear of love and relationships, which includes judgment of oneself and others

- Gift: Honoring, accepting, and loving oneself and others

The heart center relates to love and relationships. It is a feminine center. When it is in balance, we experience unconditional love, forgiveness, and compassion. When it is out of balance, our ability to experience love is replaced by judgment of ourselves and others. This is where we hold feelings of being bad, ashamed, unworthy, and so forth.

This energy center corresponds to the fourth layer of the aura, which is the spiritual bridge. Like the emotional layer, it contains all of the colors of the rainbow. In this layer, the colors are softer and usually tinted with pink, the color of love.

The Fifth or Throat Center

- Location: In the middle of the throat

- Color: Medium blue

- Corresponding Parts of the Body: The thyroid gland and the respiratory system

- Lesson: Fear of one's expression and creativity, often accompanied by an inability to bring one's inner desires into fruition

- Gift: Freely using one's expression and creativity in accordance with one's soul purpose

This masculine chakra relates to our expression and creativity. When it is functioning properly, we can communicate clearly and express ourselves appropriately. Going a step further, this is the seat of our creative expression, where we express ourselves through art, food, music, dance, and so on. When the throat chakra is out of balance, our ability to communicate is impaired, preventing us from saying what we want or blocking our ability to express ourselves in an appropriate way. Our creative expression may also be suppressed. Most of us have had the feeling of being choked up when we try to talk about something that is difficult for us. This is a sign that the energy is blocked in the throat center. This is also where the different parts of ourselves, the subpersonalities, find their expression. As we progress on the spiritual path, we integrate these fragmented parts into the wholeness of the soul, and this energy center opens.

The fifth chakra roughly corresponds to the fifth or higher physical layer of the aura, which is blue in color. This layer is a higher frequency of the first layer, which holds the energetic template for the physical body. While the template on the first layer has been distorted by the blockages on the emotional, mental, and spiritual bridge levels, the template on the fifth layer holds the undistorted blueprint that we want to bring into our physical reality.

The Sixth or Brow Center

- Location: In the center of the forehead, between the eyebrows

- Color: Dark indigo blue

- Corresponding Parts of the Body: The pituitary gland, the eyes, the ears, the lower part of the brain, and the autonomic nervous system

- Lesson: Fear of one's own vision and seeing the truth, resulting in no vision or vision distorted by the perceptions of the wounded ego

- Gift: Seeing and sharing one's clear vision in a positive and productive way

The brow chakra relates to our vision, which includes clairvoyant abilities and intuition. It is feminine. When it is in balance, our pictures of ourselves and our reality are clear and undistorted. When it is out of balance, these pictures are distorted or completely blocked. When our vision is under the control of the ego, we cannot see where our path is leading us. As we come into alignment with the soul, we can see where we want to go and easily find our way.

The saying "what you see is what you get" applies to this chakra. When we see ourselves and our possibilities as limited, our reality will reflect this distorted picture. When we are able to see unlimited possibilities, our reality reflects this clear picture. This further demonstrates the power of visualization.

This energy center roughly corresponds with the sixth or higher emotional layer of the aura. As the fifth layer is a higher frequency of the first layer, the sixth layer is a higher frequency of the second or emotional layer. It contains rainbow colors that radiate out from the body.

The Seventh or Crown Center

- Location: On the top of the head
- Color: Violet
- Corresponding Parts of the Body: The pineal gland, the upper part of the brain, and the central nervous system
- Lesson: Fear of one's own knowing and the experience of separation, often leading either to a search for knowledge outside oneself or to being a know-it-all
- Gift: Having true inner wisdom and sharing knowledge based on the experience of joy and unity

The crown chakra relates to our knowledge and divine wisdom, along with our sense of wholeness and unity. It is active and masculine. When it is in balance, we can access our inner knowing and wisdom. We also feel connected with all of life. When it is closed or out of balance, we may find ourselves in an endless search for knowledge and experience ourselves as being separate and isolated.

This center corresponds to the seventh or higher mental layer of the aura, which is a higher frequency of the third layer and yellow in color.

THE CHAKRA FOCUS

The existence of energy centers does not have to be a theoretical idea. You can learn to feel them on your body and sense what is occurring with each one in the next guided relaxation process, the Chakra Focus. Those who are familiar with such hands-on healing techniques as Reiki have probably learned to feel them on others as well.

You can use this focusing process to familiarize yourself with the energy centers or as a balancing technique, to see and feel what is occurring in each one and send healing energy where needed to balance and energize. As you explore the chakras, it is helpful to look at yourself from the perspective of a neutral observer. You could compare it to being a detective, peering into all the nooks and crannies, looking for clues to your true identity. As we have seen, our true identities are often concealed by energetic blockages that we need to release to embrace our soul. As you explore your energy centers, it can be helpful to use this detective approach, with the knowledge that under the blockages are gifts of understanding that you can give to yourself.

Start like before in a quiet, comfortable place where you will not be disturbed and where you can relax.

When you have made yourself comfortable, you can begin by taking a few deep breaths and allowing any tension you feel in your body to begin to melt away. By now you should be able to start to relax as you continue to slowly read each word and you can close your eyes any time you want to deepen the experience.

Just continue to fill your lungs with pure, clear air, and allow more tension to release with each exhale, so that with each breath, you feel more relaxed, and your body is becoming lighter and lighter, allowing the tension to melt down through your body, legs and feet and into the earth. And allow the breath to be loving and nurturing, embracing yourself with relaxation.

Now focus on breathing this clear, loving energy into your mind with each inhale, so that all of the cells of your brain can relax and any thoughts from the day can simply drift off into the air. Notice how your mind becomes more and more clear with each breath.

Allow the clear energy to flow down so that your entire head is relaxed: your forehead, your jaw and mouth, sending relaxation down your neck and shoulders, again allowing any tension in these areas to simply melt away, so your neck and shoulders can feel completely relaxed.

Now feel a wave of clear energy and relaxation moving gently down your arms, past the elbows and wrists, all the way down to the tips of your fingers. And allow another wave of relaxation to move down from your shoulders, so your entire torso can relax and all of the organs in your body can relax, moving down the chest, relaxing the lungs and heart, the stomach and down past the waist allowing all of the organs in your abdomen to relax. And now feeling the relaxation moving all the way down your spine, so that your entire back can relax, melting further into your seat. And allow the relaxation to move down the thighs, to the knees, the ankles and feet, all the way to the tips of your toes, so your entire body is relaxed and filled with clear, pure energy.

As you continue, begin to focus your breath at the base of your spine, which is the location of the base chakra. Breathe energy into this area and notice how it feels. With practice you can easily feel the energy of each chakra and begin to understand your unconscious feelings related to each one, like accessing information from a database.

The focus of the first chakra is your physical survival and well-being. As you breathe energy into this area, you can allow your feelings about your physical stability in the world to come to the surface of your awareness. If you are just becoming familiar with the chakra system, you will find that your ability to understand what is occurring in each energy center will become clearer with practice. Take a moment to notice how the energy feels in this area and what thoughts and feelings come to your awareness about your physical stability. Also allow the energy of the breath to clear any blocked energy in this chakra, so it becomes lighter and more energized with each breath. Take whatever time you need to experience the base chakra.

Now shift your awareness to the area just below your navel. This is the location of the second chakra, which focuses on your emotions and sexuality. Breathe energy and light into this area and notice how it feels. Allow your feelings about your emotions and sexuality to come to the surface. These feelings include how you feel about being nurtured and nurturing others. Take a moment to notice what comes into your awareness as you breathe energy into your second chakra and allow the breath to clear any blocked energy you feel there. Take whatever time you need to experience the navel chakra.

We will continue moving upward now as you shift the focus of your breath on the third chakra, which is located above the waist in the middle of your stomach area. This chakra focuses on our mental nature and your sense of power in the world. It is where we store our beliefs and attitudes about life and our possibilities in the world. Take a moment to notice what comes into your awareness as you breathe energy into your third chakra and allow the energy and the light of the breath to release any energetic blockages you notice here. Take whatever time you need to experience the solar plexus chakra.

The first three chakras provide information about how we relate to our physical reality: physical survival, our emotions and sexuality and our relationship to our external reality.

Now we can move up to the heart chakra. As we have seen,

in addition to being one of the seven major chakras, the heart also houses the soul. As you breathe into this area and connect with the feelings in your heart, you are also connecting with the feelings in your soul. This chakra is the bridge between our physical and spiritual worlds. It focuses on love and relationships, so as you breathe into this area, notice what feelings come up about your relationships with yourself and others and allow the energy of the breath to release any blockages you notice, so your heart area feels lighter with each breath. Take whatever time you need to experience the heart chakra.

Next, shift your awareness to your throat, which is the location of the fifth chakra. The throat chakra focuses on communication and creativity. As you breathe energy into this area, notice how you feel about your self-expression. This is the first of the three major chakras that operates at the spiritual levels. As such, it may be understood as the next higher octave of our physical expression, this time being our creative expression. Take whatever time you need to experience the throat chakra.

As we continue moving up, you can now focus your attention on the area of your forehead just above and between your eyebrows. This is the location of the sixth chakra, which focuses on your inner vision. When we discuss visualizing and your inner sight, this is the area it comes from. It is also the next higher octave of the second chakra, so it has to do with your higher emotions, which are related to unconditional love. Take a moment now to experience the brow chakra.

Now you can shift your focus to the top of your head and the seventh or crown chakra. As the higher octave of the third chakra, the crown chakra focuses on higher thought, which is your inner wisdom. It also serves as the stepping off point to the higher dimensions, so this is where we have the experience of how everything in the cosmos is connected and how spirit exists in all things. As you breathe energy into your crown chakra, notice how you feel connected with everything and everyone around you. Take whatever time you need to experience the crown chakra.

When you have finished exploring the chakras, breathe in active energy to bring yourself back to your normal state of awareness. With each breath, allow yourself to feel more alert and alive. Counting from 1 to 5, you will feel more and more alert: 1, 2, 3, feeling more awake now, 4 and 5. Now you should feel completely awake and wonderful.

Like the Heart Focus, the Chakra Focus may bring awareness to issues in one or more of the chakras that you will want to address with SK. And as with the Heart Focus, you can do a more detailed focus on any of the chakras, using imagery to uncover what is occurring. We will also explore more GTT techniques that you can use in the next section of the book.

YOUR GREATEST LESSON AND GREATEST GIFT

As you begin to understand your soul's purpose, you will discover that it represents both your greatest gift and your greatest life lesson. As a part of the divine plan, each of us is given challenges to expressing our gift. Blockages are built into our energy systems that need to be released so we can move fully into living our true joy and divine purpose. These blockages provide each of us with the opportunity to actualize our purpose with awareness.

How you can recognize your greatest lesson and gift? It is built into your energy system.

The frequency of one of the seven energy centers corresponds to the gift your soul came to share.

The energy center that represents your greatest lesson and gift also holds major lessons that weave through the smaller lessons you encounter on your path. We summarized the corresponding lessons and gifts with the descriptions of each of the chakras. Reading through the list, you may be able to recognize which center represents your greatest lesson and gift. Once you do, it usually seems obvious, but it may be hard to see at first. You can also muscle test to find out which chakra represents your greatest lesson and gift, using the question "Is the _____ chakra my greatest lesson and gift?" There should be a strong response, representing a yes, to only one of the seven chakras.

Whether you are focusing on your own spiritual path or helping others with their spiritual development, understanding a person's greatest lesson and gift provides invaluable information. As we have individual lessons that we integrate in the activation process, one's greatest lesson and greatest gift weaves through all of the other lessons, so it is a constant companion. As a person progresses through the activations and integrates more of this lesson and gift, his or her true purpose comes more into focus. Also, recognizing other peoples' lessons and gifts can help you to understand what motivates them, and how you can support them on their paths.

Knowing whether a person's greatest lesson and gift is in a masculine or feminine chakra is helpful. This orientation affects how the individual uses his or her energy. Most people have more masculine or feminine energy, and this serves their purpose. In Chapter Nine, we will discuss balancing the masculine and feminine as an integral part of the awakening process. This does not mean that each person will exhibit an equal amount of both. Some people are more feminine; others are more masculine. Regardless, each individual needs to have access to both sides to be able to fully express his or her purpose.

In his book *Life Energy*, John Diamond introduces the concept of having a homing thought. This is a thought about your purpose that you make into a summary statement. Keeping your focus on this homing thought can help you to look at all of your activities in relation to your divine purpose. Diamond states that 90 percent of workers test weak for the statement "I enjoy my work." Sadly, all of these people lose life energy just thinking about their jobs. Fortunately, it does not have to be this way. As we strengthen our relationships with our souls, we can move incrementally closer to our purpose and increase our life energy.

Diamond also has a solution. He has found that focusing on the homing thought helps an individual to remain strong in the face of adversity. He describes a client named Peter who was having difficulty in college. Testing Peter for the statement "I want to complete my present college course" produced a weak response. Unconsciously, Peter actually did not want to be in college at all. Further testing revealed that he also did not want to remain where he was currently living. Through more discussion and testing, they determined that Peter actually wanted to move to a nearby city and become a recording artist singing religious hymns. Achieving this goal became his homing thought. When focusing on it, his muscle tested strong, even after a sudden stress that would normally drain his life force and produce a weak muscle.

We have already discussed the importance of writing your goals. You can follow up on this process by distilling these goals into a statement or several statements that you can use to help you to maintain balance and to guide you toward your purpose. As you continue to change, your homing thought or guiding thought may change, too.

YOUR CURRENT LESSONS

Figure 6.2 is the Current Lessons Checklist, which you can use to identify where your current lessons are creating blockages, so you can release the imbalances with SK. Where your system is in balance, the muscle response is strong. Where there is a blockage, the muscle response is weak. You can use this handy checklist any time to locate general blockages or to help you to deal with a specific issue. It should help wherever you are on the spiritual path.

If you want to know where there are general imbalances in your energy system, use this statement: "Focus on _____," filling the blank with an item from the checklist, such as "Focus on physical survival." If you have a specific issue that you want to clear, use the following statement: "Focus on _____ (describe the imbalance) in relation to _____ (select an item from the checklist)." For instance, if you want to clear any imbalances related to a weight issue, the first statement would be: "Focus on your weight in relation to physical survival."

Here is an example. Jane was working with a client named Lynn who was dealing with a weight issue. Jane started the process by muscle testing for the first set of questions on the Current Issues checklist. Lynn tested weak for emotions, sexuality, unconditional love, communication, and wholeness and unity. This might sound like a lot of imbalances, but, as you will see, they are usually all connected, so the system returns to balance when just one or two items are addressed.

Reviewing the list of imbalances, Jane asked Lynn which one she would like to focus on. Lynn chose unconditional love, which, of course, relates to the heart center. In her heart, she felt undesirable and vulnerable to rejection. Her feelings of being undesirable started at an intensity of nine out of ten. Her heart felt weak and heavy. After one round of R&A, Lynn felt a little more self-acceptance and rated the intensity at eight.

Focusing again on the feelings of being undesirable brought tears this time. Although the first round had not shown an appreciable drop in intensity, Lynn had opened to her feelings at a deeper level. Jane understood that this was a sign of progress and encouraged Lynn to continue. Now Lynn recognized that she was dealing with unspoken rejection that she felt from her father from the time she was five. Though he never told her outright, Lynn knew that her father felt that she was not pretty enough. After a certain age, he did not touch her. Now she was feeling the unspoken rejection, which she rated at ten.

FIGURE 6.2
CURRENT LESSONS CHECKLIST

Say "Focus on _____," filling in the blank with
an item from the checklist.

The first group of statements relates directly to the lessons of the
seven energy centers.

CENTER	STATEMENT	STRONG	WEAK
1	"… physical survival."	_____	_____
2	"… emotions."	_____	_____
	"… sexuality."	_____	_____
3	"… your power in the world."	_____	_____
4	"… unconditional love."	_____	_____
	"… relationships."	_____	_____
5	"… communication."	_____	_____
	"… creativity."	_____	_____
6	"… your vision."	_____	_____
7	"… your inner knowing."	_____	_____
	"… wholeness and unity."	_____	_____

The next group of statements covers other aspects of our reality.

STATEMENT	STRONG	WEAK
"… reaching out in your life."	_____	_____
"… moving forward in your life."	_____	_____
"… feeling grounded and present in your life."	_____	_____
"… following your soul's path."	_____	_____

After just one round of R&A, Lynn's feelings of rejection were gone completely. Her heart felt lighter, and she could tell that she was still clearing. They muscle tested for unconditional love again, but she still tested weak. She realized that she felt more love for herself, but felt undesirable as a woman. The feelings of being undesirable were still at an eight, so they did another round of R&A, which brought them down to zero. Now Lynn knew that when the right person came along, he would love her entire being.

Returning once more to the muscle testing, all of items that were out of balance when they started now tested strong, and they knew the process was complete.

Lynn's inspiring example shows how easily we can release limitations that prevent us from recognizing the magnificence of ourselves and our souls. Armed with knowledge and practical tools for connecting with your soul, now we will take out the third key and focus on uncovering your soul's expression.

BECOMING AN EXPRESSION OF YOUR SOUL

CHAPTER SEVEN

Uncovering Your Soul's Expression

*All animals except man
know that the ultimate of life
is to enjoy it.*

–SAMUEL BUTLER

With knowledge of the Seven Spiritual Activations, you may be wondering where to go from here. This part of the book focuses on provides healing techniques that you can use to move forward and uncover your soul's expression.

During the first three stages of our spiritual development, we gradually integrate new levels of understanding of our spiritual identities. As mentioned previously, the first stage generally goes by relatively unnoticed. Awareness of the existence of the spiritual path and the conscious desire to follow it usually arises in the second or third stage, as the wounded ego begins to loosen its hold.

In these initial stages, there is a wide gap between the soul's awareness and our daily awareness. This is normal. As we progress on the journey, the wounded ego starts to heal and the soul's presence gains strength. The gap narrows, until it largely disappears. In the meantime, if you experience such gaps, using guiding thoughts and positive affirmations can help. Repeating them and writing them on notes on the refrigerator, the bathroom mirror, your desk, and similar places can help you to remember your true identity more often.

With the Fourth Activation, the process of awakening usually moves fully to the forefront, as we strive to embrace the wounded parts of ourselves. By this point, we have severed our connections with the mass consciousness, recognized our individuality, and claimed some of our power. It is during this stage that the soul's presence overcomes the ego's dominance. Now, with the soul directing us, we venture into the unknown.

A GUIDE TO THE GTT PROCESSES

In this part of the book, we present more of the GTT processes that we use with each other, our clients and students. We actually started in Chapter Three, where we presented the Soul Centering Process and Chapter Four, where we presented the Heart Focus. To provide an overview, Figure 7.1 describes all of the GTT processes in this book. Because of their holistic nature, all of these techniques can be helpful at any stage and with any healing process. If you are not sure which one to use, you can muscle test with the question "Is _____ the right process to use now (or to use with this issue)?"

We developed the Getting Thru Techniques (GTT) to connect with ourselves and others in a more profound way. You have already seen how you can clear many energetic blockages with Spiritual Kinesiology without having full awareness of what is happening in the unconscious mind. This makes enlightenment much easier to attain. Sometimes you may want to know more, which is where GTT comes in.

We will use the GTT processes with SK, or EFT, if you pre-

FIGURE 7.1
OVERVIEW OF THE GTT PROCESSES

You can use the Getting Thru Techniques as a starting point with any issue or if you are not having success with SK or EFT. Here is an overview of each of the processes.

PROCESS	RECOMMENDED USE
Chapter 3: Soul Centering Process	The Soul Centering Process provides a soul connection that can then serve as a resource for clearing blockages and bringing a higher level of awareness and understanding to any question or issue.
Chapter 4: Heart Focus	The Heart Focus provides a way for you to access the feelings you hold in your heart through a guided visualization. You can use it with or without having a specific issue in mind. The imagery can reveal blockages to your soul's expression, as well as how you have progressed on the path.
Chapter 7: Illumination Process	This process explores the Seven Levels of Healing, so you can understand how an issue is affecting you emotionally, mentally, and spiritually. It includes the use of imagery to enhance your awareness, and either SK or EFT to clear blockages.
Chapter 8: Integration Process	This process helps you to directly contact the subpersonality who is involved with any issue you want to address and includes the use of imagery. It also includes the use of either SK or EFT to clear the blockages you encounter.
Chapter 9: Integration Meeting	The Integration Meeting is a role-playing technique that helps you to connect with any polarized parts of yourself that need healing. It includes the use of your soul's wisdom and the optional use of SK or EFT to bring these parts back into alignment with the soul.

fer, so that you can clear the blockages quickly and easily. Also, GTT usually works when you are not getting satisfactory results with SK or EFT alone. In such cases, there is usually something you need to understand consciously to clear the pattern. The GTT processes we present in this book can help you to bring more of your soul's wisdom to any kind of problem.

THE THREE STEPS IN ANY HEALING PROCESS

As we explore our inner worlds and develop a more unified understanding of ourselves and our souls, we grow personally and spiritually. Gradually we return to a sense of wholeness. There are three basic steps in any healing processes we experience on the journey: clearing, integrating, and activating.

1. **Clearing:** We start any healing process with the awareness that something is wrong. This may be physical, emotional, mental, or spiritual. The clearing process releases the blockages, preparing us to embrace more light and soul awareness.

2. **Integrating:** Once clearing has occurred, there is a period of restructuring or integrating. With the clearing, a blockage has been released. Now our energetic makeup shifts to accommodate more spiritual light and conscious awareness. This integration process may take hours, days, weeks, maybe even months, depending on the nature of the blockage. It is largely a process of experiencing the soul in a more expanded way, and allowing the limiting patterns to release.

3. **Activating:** The last step is activating a greater awareness of oneself. In each of our lives, the soul determines when we are ready to let in more light and to activate a more expanded level of consciousness. As we have seen, there are seven major activations, which are like milestones on the spiritual path. There are also a many minor activations that correspond with each of the individual healing processes we undertake.

Once these three steps are complete, the process begins again, like a spiral. The light from the activation shines on other dark areas and new issues come up to be cleared. Gradually, we notice that life is different; it becomes richer as we spiral upward and integrate more of the soul's light.

Understanding the healing process helps us to recognize the importance of clearing and integrating. Some individuals on the spiritual path strive to build light without making the effort to detect and clear the energetic blockages that become exposed. This avoidance creates a backup, much like a sewer, which builds over time and prevents the individual from progressing further in the activation process. Like a sewer, people in this situation are difficult to be around because of the build up of negativity. They also tend to spend a lot of their energy on denying the lessons that are before them. Fortunately, with an open mind and the proper tools, this does not need to occur.

Even those whose family lives and/or occupations are in alignment with their purposes need to increase their awareness to become expressions of their souls and, ultimately, to co-create. Take the example of a schoolteacher whose greatest lesson and gift are in his fifth chakra. Teaching may be his divine purpose, but he still needs to complete the stages in his development for his soul to be able to freely express itself through his teaching. Similarly, a mother with a second chakra gift needs to bring awareness to her lessons and gifts for her soul to freely express itself through mothering.

THE SEVEN LEVELS OF HEALING

If we continue to focus on the journey, and what the events of our lives are here to teach us, we can appreciate our challenges and make rapid progress by clearing the blockages that come up. As mentioned earlier, each blockage in the unconscious mind also represents an energetic blockage imprinted in the energy field and the chakra system. They manifest as feelings of inadequacy, limited beliefs, painful emotions, and health problems. When these problems come to our attention, the soul is telling us that it is time to examine and release them.

The Seven Levels of Healing provide a clear picture of how energetic blockages develop and how to heal them.

Understanding how our issues and corresponding blockages relate to the seven levels of the aura can facilitate healing and spiritual growth. A blockage in the mind generally corresponds to blockages in each of the seven levels. We have already seen that these blockages equate to dark areas in the aura, where energy does not flow. As we bring awareness to an issue and learn the lesson it is here to teach, the energetic blockages in the seven levels are released. The dark areas become lighter and energy flows more freely.

The Seven Levels of Healing is an extension of the Four Levels of Healing we presented in the Holistic Process in *Getting Thru to Your Emotions with EFT*. There, we explored the physical, emotional, mental, and spiritual levels. Here we are adding the higher physical, higher emotional, and higher mental levels that we integrate on the spiritual journey.

We use the Seven Levels of Healing as a roadmap for all of our clearing work. This is where the movement to joy, love, and freedom comes in. On the first level, healing provides physical well-being. On the second or emotional level, there is movement from fear and negative emotions to joy. On the mental level, it is a movement from ignorance in the form of limiting beliefs and attitudes to unlimited thinking, which provides genuine power and freedom. On the fourth level, it is a movement from judgment and separation to acceptance and unconditional love. From the perspective of your expression on the fifth level, you are moving from expression of the fragmented parts of the personality to the clear expression of the soul. In the process, your vision, on the sixth level, which was distorted by the blockage, becomes clear. And on the seventh level, you reconnect with the truth of your soul and your awareness of how you are connected with all of life.

TRACKING BLOCKAGES IN THE AURA

With knowledge of how energy moves through the aura, you have a powerful tool for your spiritual growth. The energy field is holistic in nature. The seven levels map out the levels of our reality that we address in any healing process. We represent these levels in Figure 7.2 as The Seven Levels of Healing.

When Jane first heard about the aura, she, like many others, assumed that it is a reflection of the physical body. This is based on the presumption that the physical body is the most "real." Through our work, we have come to understand that it is actually the opposite. The physical body is a reflection of the energy field. And energetic blockages enter the aura from the outside, so they appear first in the seventh layer. The blockage then moves inward through the layers to the physical body. This is why a holistic approach to any condition is needed for complete and lasting success. Each blockage has physical, emotional, mental, and spiritual components.

When we experience ourselves as whole, unified, and connected with the source, we are unaffected by blockages.

Looking again at the seventh layer, blockages in the aura develop when we lose that sense of connectedness and wholeness. This is when the split occurs, separating a part of the self from the soul. From there, the blockage moves in through the layers, which correspond with the chakras in reverse order, seven through one. Figure 7.3 illustrates The Seven Levels of the Energy Field and how imbalances enter and leave the aura. We will go through each of the levels, so that you can understand the sequence.

FIGURE 7.2
THE SEVEN LEVELS OF HEALING

On the seven levels of our reality, the healing process and the spiritual journey lead us from the limitations of the wounded ego to the light and wisdom of the soul. Here is what happens at each level.

1. ETHERIC LEVEL
Lesson of Physical Survival
From pain, discomfort and illness . . . . to health and well-being

2. EMOTIONAL LEVEL
Lesson of Emotions and Sexuality
From fear and painful emotions . . . . to joy and positive emotions

3. MENTAL LEVEL
Lesson of Power in the World
From limiting beliefs . . . . to unlimited thinking and freedom

4. SPIRITUAL BRIDGE LEVEL
Lesson of Love and Relationships
From judgment of self and others . . . . to love and acceptance

5. HIGHER PHYSICAL LEVEL
Lesson of Expression and Creativity
From expression of wounded ego . . . . to expression of soul

6. HIGHER EMOTIONAL LEVEL
Lesson of Vision
From distorted vision . . . . . . to clear vision in alignment with purpose

7. HIGHER MENTAL LEVEL
Lesson of Knowledge and Wholeness
From disconnected from truth . . . . . to strong sense of truth and unity

---

FIGURE 7.3
THE SEVEN LEVELS OF THE ENERGY FIELD

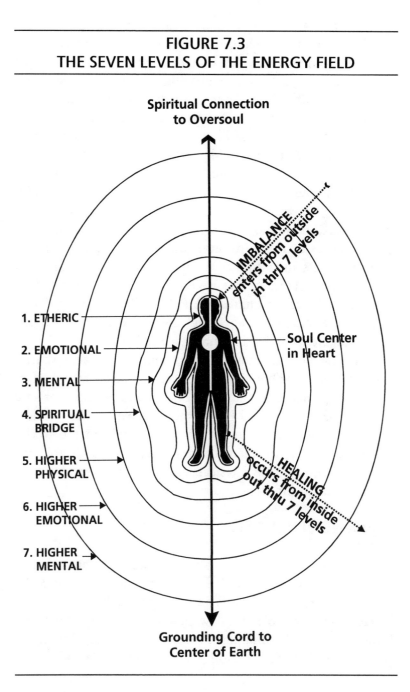

Spiritual Connection
to Oversoul

IMBALANCE
enters from outside
in thru 7 levels

1. ETHERIC

2. EMOTIONAL

3. MENTAL

4. SPIRITUAL
BRIDGE

5. HIGHER
PHYSICAL

6. HIGHER
EMOTIONAL

7. HIGHER
MENTAL

Soul Center
in Heart

HEALING
occurs from inside
out thru 7 levels

Grounding Cord to
Center of Earth

Once we have lost our connectedness and sense of wholeness in the seventh level, the blockage moves to the sixth level, relating to our vision, which becomes distorted. We no longer experience ourselves as unified with the whole. We see ourselves as disconnected and our vision becomes painful.

From there it moves to the fifth level and our expression. As a part of the self is disowned, our expression becomes blocked. We are no longer able to be a clear expression of the soul. We become an expression of fragmented parts of the ego.

Then the blockage goes to the fourth level, creating judgment. We no longer recognize ourselves a soul in a state of perfection. Instead, we judge ourselves as flawed or inadequate.
This leads us to the third level, where the judgments create limiting beliefs and attitudes about our power in the world. Instead of understanding that we are free to create, we believe that many things are impossible. Beliefs like "life is difficult" or "I'll never amount to anything" are external manifestations of the judgments we hold about ourselves.

Then the blockage moves to the second level, where we find fears and negative emotions, often not knowing why we feel them; and, finally, to the first level, which is the energetic template for the physical body, where we experience physical sensations and the ability to feel comfortable in the world. When we become fragmented, we become uncomfortable; we want to escape. At the physical level, this fragmentation can also manifest as illness or injury.

CLEARING BLOCKAGES

To clear the blockages in the aura, you want to track them in the opposite order, from the innermost level outward, by bringing awareness to what is happening at each level.

Here is an example of following a lesson through the seven layers with the Illumination Process, which follows. A client we will call Alan came to Phillip with a problem he was having at work. A new co-worker named Judith had recently replaced a person with whom Alan had had a close working relationship. Alan likewise started out working in a spirit of trust and cooperation with Judith. But after several unsettling incidents, Alan felt that his trust had been misplaced. Judith was manipulating him behind the scenes. Alan gave the example of how she would violate his directions by editing the ads he had given her before submitting them to the local paper. She did this repeatedly, sometimes adding information that would benefit her personally.

Alan wanted to resolve his inner conflict, so Phillip recommended using the Illumination Process. Here is a summary of what they found at each level:

- Physically, Alan felt discomfort in his solar plexus, which usually relates to the third chakra and one's sense of power.

- At the emotional level, Alan felt frustrated.

- The mental level evoked thoughts that the integrity of the business was being undermined. When Phillip asked Alan to explain this further, Alan realized that he also believed his personal integrity was being undermined.

- At the spiritual bridge level, Alan felt that he had become mired in a mistake.

- At the higher physical level, which corresponds to expression and creativity, Alan felt shut down and defensive.

- At the higher emotional level, which relates to vision, Phillip asked Alan to visualize the issue as a landscape. Alan pictured downtown Los Angeles, which he described as the opposite of a peaceful, natural scene. The city was rushed and fearful, filled with traffic, concrete, and disruptive energy.

- The higher mental level, which relates to truth and inner knowing, found him confused and at a loss.

Alan noted the intensity of his frustration to be about six out of ten. One round of Reframing and Anchoring quickly brought the intensity down to one. Alan felt it was continuing to release as the process unfolded.

Taking another look, Alan's landscape had been transformed by the process. The city was gone, replaced by a natural setting. Alan now visualized himself walking in a forest, with sunlight filtering through the leaves, amid sounds of chirping birds. A waterfall cascaded in the distance.

With Phillip's guidance, Alan again examined the layers of his energy field, On the physical level, Alan's solar plexus was now comfortable and his body felt energized. Emotionally, he noted that his frustration was gone. Mentally, he believed that he was not compromised by anyone outside of himself. Spiritually, he felt inner peace. The former troubling situation was no longer a conflict. At the fifth level, Alan felt his creative expression had been cleaned and restored. Having transformed his distorted vision on the sixth level, they finished the process with the seventh level, where he experienced expansion and freedom. Afterward, Alan said he was amazed that such a serious conflict could be resolved so easily.

THE ILLUMINATION PROCESS

As mentioned earlier, we presented a GTT technique called the Holistic Process in *Getting Thru to Your Emotions with EFT*, where we addressed the first four levels of the aura. Phillip's book *Getting Thru to Kids* provides an easy-to-use five-step process that describes how you can uncover these levels with children and help them to participate in problem-solving.

For your spiritual development, the Illumination Process provides imagery, addresses all seven levels and provides deep spiritual healing. You can use it with any conflict to understand how it is reflected in the different levels of your reality. To complete the clearing part of the process, you need to be familiar with SK and Soul Centering. As an alternative, you can use EFT.

Figure 7.4 is a guide for Mapping the Seven Levels of Healing. As you go through each one, we recommend recording what you discover in this format, to pinpoint all of the details. Before starting, you also need to identify a single issue that you want to examine and define it clearly in your mind.

As you go through the seven levels, holding your focus on your thoughts and feelings related to each level is a key to your success. You do not want to digress into how it would be if you did not have the issue. Most people connect relatively easily with the sensations in the body and the emotions related to an issue. The limiting beliefs and judgments, however, are usually buried in the deeper recesses of the unconscious mind, which also are more vulnerable.

When they reach these and the higher levels, some people disconnect from the sensations and emotions that will lead them to the unconscious beliefs, judgments, and spiritual levels. Instead, they cover their vulnerability with positive affirmations, saying that they feel fine and that they can handle the problem. Affirmations are a wonderful tool, but this is not the time to use them. The purpose of this process is to uncover the truth of what you are experiencing at each level and to heal each one. You need to stay with these experiences for the process to be complete.

Now, as you keep your focus on the issue at hand, you are ready to begin.

Start by bringing your problem fully into your awareness and allow your mind to take you to a time when this issue was difficult for you. This may be a time in the recent past, or your mind may take you to a time further back in time, maybe even to your childhood. Whenever it is, focus on your experience at that time. Close your eyes for a moment, and focus on your experience.

Now notice how your body feels as you continue to focus on the issue. Sometimes, the physical sensations may be subtle; at

FIGURE 7.4
MAPPING THE SEVEN LEVELS OF HEALING

BEFORE:

Start by identifying a single issue to address.

Write down what is happening on each level before clearing.

Level 1: Physical Sensations

Level 2: Emotions

Level 3: Beliefs

Level 4: Judgments

Level 5: Expression and Creativity

Level 6: Vision

Level 7: Knowledge and Wholeness

FIGURE 7.4
CONTINUED

AFTER:

Write down what is happening on each level after clearing.

Level 1: Physical Sensations

_____

_____

Level 2: Emotions

_____

_____

Level 3: Beliefs

_____

_____

Level 4: Judgments

_____

_____

Level 5: Expression and Creativity

_____

_____

Level 6: Vision

_____

_____

_____

Level 7: Knowledge and Wholeness

_____

_____

Summary: How do you feel about the problem after you are done?

_____

_____

other times, they may be strong. You may just experience tightness somewhere in your body or a change in your breathing. Close your eyes for a moment, and notice how your body feels as you continue to focus on your issue. Then write down what you noticed physically as "Level 1: Physical Sensations." If you did not notice anything, make a note of that, too.

Next, allow your awareness to move to the emotions that lie behind the physical sensations. Imagining that you are breathing energy into the sensations can help you to connect with the emotions that are behind them. If you did not notice anything at the physical level, just focus on bringing up the emotions related to your issue. As you do this, you may uncover more than one emotion. Notice the first emotion that comes into your awareness, and allow yourself to understand what it relates to. Then, ask yourself if there are any other emotions that you need to explore. You may want to close your eyes again for a few moments and explore the emotions by continuing to focus on the issue and allowing each one to surface until you reach the deepest emotion. Record the emotions you noticed as "Level 2: Emotions."

Next, focus on the deepest emotion and ask yourself how that emotion makes you feel about your possibilities in the world. If you are not sure which is the deepest, just focus on any of the emotions. Here you will find the limiting beliefs and attitudes that exist at the mental level. You may want to close your eyes again for a moment and focus on how you feel limited in the outside world in relation to your issue. Write down the limiting beliefs and attitudes as "Level 3: Beliefs."

Next, focus again on the beliefs and attitudes, and ask how they make you feel about yourself. This brings out the judgments, which are the limited ways we understand ourselves when we see ourselves as being separate from the wholeness and unity of life. As with the emotions and beliefs, there may be more than one judgment. You may wish to close your eyes and focus on how you feel about yourself in relation to your issue. When you have finished, write down the judgments as "Level 4: Judgments."

In exploring these four levels, we have been exploring characteristics of a part of you who has become separated from the light of your soul. Now ask yourself how this problem has effected your self-expression and creativity. Record how this level has been effected as "Level 5: Expression and Creativity."

On the next level are the images that relate to the problem. If you were to imagine a landscape that represents the problem you are experiencing, what would it be? Involve all of your senses. Notice the details of the scene: the colors, shapes, the appearance of the sky, the earth, and any other features of the landscape. Notice any sounds and how the landscape feels both physically and emotionally. As you visualize the scene, write down what you see under "Level 6: Vision."

Finally, as you continue to focus on your problem, notice how you feel about your own knowing and about your connection with those around you. Write down these feelings under "Level 7: Knowledge and Wholeness."

Now you are ready to use SK or EFT. As you continue to focus on the emotion or issue, measure the intensity of the experience from one to ten. Next, you can clear the imbalance. Instructions here use SK, but you may substitute EFT. To use the R&A technique, focus again on the problem and place your left hand on your left knee to anchor the experience. Count silently to ten as you continue to focus on the problem, then release your hand.

Now take a couple of deep breaths like before, setting aside the thoughts of your issue as you focus on your breathing. With each breath, allow yourself to relax more, so any tension in your body can melt away and drift gently down into the earth. Notice that even as you continue reading, you can go into a pleasant state of relaxation, guided by your breath.

As you relax, imagine the light above your head, and allow the perfect energy to come down from your higher self to clear the imbalance. Feel the energy flowing in through the top of your head, filling your body with its light, then filling all of the space around you. When you feel strong and balanced by this energy, place your right hand on your right knee to anchor the new pattern and, taking another deep breath, feel this energy becoming even stronger, bringing perfect understanding of your issue. As you continue to feel your soul's energy strengthen, count to ten, then release your hand. If you were not able to connect with the energy of your higher self, focus on a time when you felt strong and good, and anchor that energy.

Now allow your mind to clear. Place your right and left hands on both anchors and count to ten, then remove your left hand from the left knee. Count to five while leaving the right hand on the right knee, then release the right hand.

Now take a few nice, deep breaths as your energy system reconfigures. When you are ready, return to the landscape you visualized earlier and notice how it has changed. Involve all of your senses again, focusing on the same features of the scene that you noticed before. If SK balanced the issue, there should be some differences now. As you continue to focus on the scene, measure any emotional intensity you feel now between one and ten.

If necessary, you can repeat the balancing process. Remember that it is normal for it to take a few rounds of Reframing and Anchoring to clear an issue completely. As you repeat the process, notice how the landscape changes with each round.

When you have finished the Reframing and Anchoring, review what you wrote for each of the levels and notice how your perspective has changed. Then write a new list and document your current experience at each level. This will help you to integrate the changes you have experienced.

As the process closes, connect with the energy of your soul in your heart and ask if there are any final messages on this issue.

Now focus on coming back fully into the present moment. As you do, feel how you are connected with everything around you. Allow a new sense of wholeness to permeate your being. Breathe in active, waking energy. Notice yourself feeling more and more alert with each breath, and come back with a new level of understanding of yourself.

Here is an example of using the Illumination Process with the Current Lesson Checklist. Jane was working with a client named Julia who wanted to know where there were imbalances in her energy system. They went through the muscle tests on the Current Lessons Checklist in Figure 6.1. The item that created the weakest muscle responses was her emotions.

Muscle testing often evokes an understanding of what the difficulties are. Julia told Jane that she was afraid of her feelings and often discounted them. She recalled being an expressive child and how this expressiveness frightened her parents. She learned to subdue her emotions to get along with them.

Seeing an opportunity to clear the blockage with the Illumination Process, Jane asked Julia where she felt the fear in her body. Julia felt a knot and a sense of anxiety in her stomach that was not there before. Having uncovered the fear on the emotional level, they went on to the mental level. Julia said that believed that if she really followed her feelings, someone would hold her back. On the spiritual bridge level, this caused her to doubt her value, feeling like she might be on the wrong track. She said that maybe others were right. Maybe their fears would come true. Maybe she would not fit in, or maybe society would harm her in some way.

Jane then asked Julia what her fear would look like if she imagined it as a landscape. Julia saw a desolate area with a big hole in the middle of it. Everything was dry, and the earth had craters in it. Asked how it would sound there, Julia said that it would be a low, hollow drone.

At that point, Julia estimated her fear to be around five out of ten. After doing a round of Reframing and Anchoring, it was down to a two. The landscape was changing, too. Julia noted that flowers and grass were trying to come up through the dry earth. The hole had filled in, leaving a slight indentation in the ground. After another round of R&A, the fear was less than one. The indentation in the earth was even smaller and there were trees in the landscape. Although it was still a little dry, it was looking much better. With one more round of R&A, the fear was just about gone. As a note, the Finger Rolling Technique would probably have worked equally well for releasing the last traces of the emotion.

Now Julia saw water in the landscape, along with lots of trees, grass, and multi-colored flowers. There were no indentations in the earth and she could hear birds chirping and the sound of a gentle breeze. Retracing the Levels of Healing, the burning knot was gone from Julia's stomach. On the mental level, she knew that she could accomplish what she wanted, that she was being directed by a higher power and protected. Spiritually, she now saw that others fears are their limitations and that they do not have to affect her. She felt complete and her arm tested strong when she focused on emotions.

Reading this example, you may have noticed that Jane did not ask Julia to focus on all seven levels. Once you have familiarized yourself with the Illumination Process, you can abbreviate the steps in some cases. In Julia's case, Jane knew that the imbalance existed primarily at the emotional level from the muscle testing. Along with the emotional level, she traced the imbalance at the physical, mental, and spiritual bridge levels. From there, the visualization completed the picture. Following the idea that "what you see is what you get," the image told the whole story. When the landscape had completed its transformation, Jane knew that the process was complete.

A NOTE ON PHYSICAL CONDITIONS

We have had amazing success helping people with physical conditions to deal with the related emotions, beliefs, and judgments that can interfere with the healing process. Using SK, EFT or GTT to deal with these emotions can help to enlist the support of the unconscious mind and stimulate the body's ability to heal.

As spiritual counselors, we do not recommend substituting

the processes in this book for professional medical treatment, when needed. Sometimes people on the spiritual path feel that they should be able to deal with their medical problems without the assistance of doctors. We have seen people respond wonderfully when combining necessary medical procedures like surgery with the understanding of the Illumination Process. It is gratifying to see them recover quickly from medical treatment, while receiving a spiritual boost from the release of the imbalance that was held in the body or in the energy field.

In one such case, a client named Theresa had sinus surgery to deal with a deviated septum. As a child, her father had hit her on the nose and caused the damage. Emotional clearing obviously could not correct the structural problem with the nose. When she had the surgery, Theresa found more layers of emotional pain came up to be released. As she healed, she felt that the surgery brought up trauma that had been held in her body for many years. When the trauma was released using EFT and GTT, she healed quickly. The procedure was a complete success that would not have been possible without both the surgery and the Illumination Process.

Now you have an overview of holistic healing and the human energy field. In the next chapter, we will change our perspective and explore the wounded parts of ourselves that need to be healed, so we can live our divine purpose.

CHAPTER EIGHT

Working with Subpersonalities

Be a lamp unto yourself.
Hold the truth within yourself.

–BUDDHA

Another powerful way to clear imbalances is to work directly with the fragmented parts of ourselves, the subpersonalities. These fragmented parts represent blockages to the soul's expression. They are the parts of us who experience the judgments, limiting beliefs, and unresolved emotions we strive to overcome in our return to wholeness.

THE ORIGINS OF THE SUBPERSONALITIES

Normally, when we think of ourselves as "I," we assume that each of us is a unified person with one viewpoint and a complete understanding of ourselves. This perception is a distortion of the ego. In reality, our mixed emotions and conflicting desires are continually showing us that we have many diverse parts within us. These subpersonalities have developed as the result of difficult or traumatic events, along with the conditioning of our society and peers. In each case, there is a pairing of a recognized part, which we are able to acknowledge consciously, and a disowned part, which we are unable to acknowledge, and which is hidden in the unconscious.

With awareness, you can probably begin to recognize these different parts of yourself. An extreme example is what psychologists call multiple personality disorder, which happens when the events of a person's life, particularly in childhood, are so severe that the subpersonalities function as separate people. In most of us, the fragmentation is subtler; we think we are one individual, but different parts of ourselves take over in different situations. You may have noticed this when a person you know suddenly withdraws, behaves childishly, or becomes fearful. In such cases, a part has come forward who is dealing with a distressing situation as best it can. These parts may seem exaggerated or inappropriate, but each one has a positive intent and aims to help.

Our subpersonalities create unconscious responses to the world and imaginary limitations about what we can and cannot do or can and cannot become. We have all had experiences when we did not understand why we behaved in a certain way, or why we suddenly became afraid or aggressive. With all of this unconscious activity, it may be very difficult if not impossible to reach our goals. It certainly makes it hard to follow the soul's path, which is our true calling and greatest joy.

An interesting exercise that can help you to understand what may be hidden in your unconscious is to write down what kind of person you consider yourself to be. Where we lack awareness, our ideas of ourselves are like masks that we wear that hide us from the disowned parts of ourselves. For example, a woman who considers herself to be a likable person may hide from the parts that she would consider to be less likable. Or a man who considers himself to be strong and impermeable may hide from the parts of himself that are vulnerable. In the process of awakening, we have to remove these masks and integrate each of these disowned parts into our awareness.

CULTURAL INFLUENCES

The parts of oneself who are acknowledged or disowned may relate to the culture a person lives in. For example, in some societies it is acceptable for men to express their emotions and cry, whereas, in our society this is generally considered a sign of weakness. In Chapter One, we discussed how our culture, which focuses largely on accomplishment, values masculine qualities more than feminine ones, such as intuition, loving, and nurturing. For this reason, the feminine half of both men and women is often disowned. On a related note, sometimes a person will rebel and develop qualities that are the opposite of the norm for his culture. This is just the other side of the coin and not to be mistaken for a higher level of consciousness.

Working with our subpersonalities allows us to return to the wholeness of the soul.

The fragmented parts of ourselves have developed over a period of years and, in some cases, over many lifetimes. Each of us has been rewarded for some behaviors, punished for others, and fragmented by traumatic experiences.

THE WOUNDED INNER CHILD

Many of our subpersonalities come from the impressionable time of our childhood. Children are highly programmable, particularly in the first seven years of life. Difficult or traumatic experiences from these early years frequently create blockages that stay for life. Also, any input a child receives from a parent, teacher, or peer has the potential of being taken at face value as an absolute truth by the unconscious mind of an impressionable child. This programming follows the child into adulthood. As a result, most of us go through life with self-imposed limitations that are based on situations that we have completely forgotten. The unconscious mind, however, never forgets and will continue to respond as best it can until the programming is changed.

It is even common for people to be affected by trauma that occurred before they were born. Carl Carpenter describes this phenomenon: "We find that many of the distresses that break down our emotional and immune systems started at the time of the conception and before the birth. In most cases, when we erase the energy created at that time [with Hypno-Kinesiology], changes take place naturally." Because of the physical connection in the womb, we pick up feelings from our parents at the time of conception and in the womb. If the mother felt anger, fear, hatred, or guilt, these feelings may become a part of the child's programming. We have seen numerous examples of adults who were still suffering from trauma such as an awareness of being unwanted or placing a financial hardship for the family, both of which started before birth.

The time of birth is also poignant. As one of the most important events our lives, it is also one of the times when we are the most programmable. And, until recently, our society's approach to childbirth has completely overlooked the baby's experience, treating him or her as a thing more than a person. This can be devastating to the newborn, who is making his or her grand entry into the world.

An example of birth trauma is a client we will call Gloria, who was embarking on a career doing healing work and spiritual teaching. She was having trouble with long-held attitudes of distrust and hostility toward others. These attitudes were obviously not harmonious with her chosen career, so she wanted to understand more about what was happening in her unconscious mind. Through her work with Jane, Gloria discovered that she had birth trauma. She recalled being stuck in the birth canal and removed with forceps. Her memory of the experience was that the medical team was uncaring and insensitive to her pain. In addition to the resulting distrust and hostility, she had carried neck and shoulder pain all of her life. Once she was able to release the distressing emotions with Jane's assistance, the pain improved too.

These types of difficulties may come from any time in childhood. In recent years, awareness of the importance of the inner child has become widespread, thanks to people like John Bradshaw, the popular author of *Homecoming: Reclaiming and Championing Your Inner Child*. Bradshaw has developed some effective techniques for working with the wounded inner child. The basis of this work is that each of us has blockages that are directly connected with painful childhood experiences, and this wounded inner child remains with us unconsciously, waiting for us to acknowledge him or her and heal the wounds.

When the child has been wounded, part of a person's emotional, mental, and spiritual development may be arrested. A thirty-year-old may be six years old on the emotional, mental, and spiritual levels. Carl Carpenter addresses inner child development in *The Far Side of Hypno-Kinesiology*:

> If the inner child is immature, it affects the person's self-confidence, self-esteem, and ability to withstand emotional pressure.... I also believe that these emotional blocks impede our spiritual growth. Spiritual changes take place when the child within is matured. If, at conception and before birth, there are no emotional blocks, we will mature at the same rate as the spiritual being. We can then find our spiritual path and follow it freely. If there is a block, there is no integration of the spirit and the person. There will be constant conflict between the spirit guidance system and the human being.

PAST LIFE PERSONALITIES

While exploring subpersonalities, you may also encounter a

fragmented part of yourself from a past life. Interestingly enough, you do not have to believe in past lives to work successfully with these fragmented parts. All you need is an open mind. As you begin to do subpersonality work, you may encounter wounded parts of yourself that are not from your current life. You have the choice of viewing them and the events they show you as metaphors, which they may be in some cases. Fortunately, to integrate the disowned parts, you only need to understand what the issues are, not whether your experience is factually accurate.

Nonetheless, it may help to recognize that the belief in reincarnation has a long tradition in both Eastern and Western faiths. The most well-known are the eastern beliefs like Hinduism and Buddhism; even western faiths like Judaism and early Christianity included references to reincarnation. It wasn't until the 4th century A.D. that these references were removed from New Testament, presumably to maintain the church's autonomy. Even now, more than 50 percent of the people in the United States believe in life after death.

The soul has access to all of the information about our past, which is stored in the unconscious mind. Sometimes blockages from traumatic events or belief systems from these lives have stayed with us and are affecting our current life. This is why accessing these past events is so helpful and illuminating.

You may wonder how accurate a person's past life recall actually is. From our observations of students and clients, we have concluded that they produce a combination of fact, metaphor, and imagination. Percentages may vary, depending on how much the individual is prepared to understand consciously about a given issue, and how honest the person is able to be with his- or herself. The ego may want to see itself as a king, queen, or other famous historical figure, when most of our past lives are relatively ordinary. Technically, accuracy does not matter, but a soulful desire for honesty does. The important thing is in the message the unconscious mind wants to convey. For the purposes of our spiritual development, we do not really need to distinguish fact from fiction.

Past life personalities can provide the key to understanding many aspects of our lives, including physical conditions, psychological tendencies, emotions, habits, food preferences, and tastes in clothing. Blockages from a past life or lives may be the source of current problems. Past life trauma creates energetic blockages to fully expressing ourselves just as childhood trauma does. Past life experiences may also provide keys to problems we are having in relationships, as people may be together in this life to resolve conflicts from the past. If you feel that someone you encounter as you review an experience from another time reminds you of someone you know now, this may indicate that you knew each other in another life.

THE GOAL OF SUBPERSONALITY WORK

The goal in doing subpersonality work is to accept all of the parts of ourselves unconditionally. This relates most directly to the Fourth Activation, Embracing, which is when we address many of our inner child and past life issues. Subpersonality work is helpful during all of the other stages, too, as we integrate more and more parts of our souls into our lives.

Jane once had a dream that helped her to understand the process of integrating the disowned parts of herself. Throughout her life, she had been troubled by dreams of being chased by monsters and evil-looking people. There were variations, but in each dream she would hide, knowing that her pursuer would find her.

The last dream in this series occurred a few years ago. In this dream, Jane was outside at night walking her dog. As she returned home, she realized that a stranger was following her. Frightened, she ducked into a nearby car, feeling that he would inevitably find her. She waited and, sure enough, his face appeared in the window. This ended the dream.

In reviewing the dream with a visualization technique, Jane returned to the climax, when the stranger appeared in the window. This time she looked directly at him and asked what he wanted. As she did, Jane understood that he represented the parts of herself that she had not accepted. She sent him love, knowing that she would not be troubled by these dreams again.

The stranger in this dream represented what Jane understood as her karma. The difficult experiences we attract with others, which some people call karmic, help us to integrate the disowned parts of ourselves.

> ### *Once we accept all of the parts of ourselves unconditionally, we are no longer troubled by karma.*

Accepting ourselves includes both the parts who have been wronged and the parts who have done or are capable of doing wrong to others. We do not have to be aware of all of the things we have done in the past, but we need to be able to observe the cruel and unjust aspects of humanity with compassion and without judgment, understanding that they also represent parts of ourselves who we now accept.

THE INTEGRATION PROCESS

There are many ways to access subpersonalities. We presented the Unification Process in *Getting Thru to Your Emotions with EFT*. This process connects you with a subpersonality; it then allows you to clear the blockages you encounter with EFT and re-unify the fragmented part. The Integration Process is similar, using either SK or EFT to integrate the disowned part with the wholeness of the soul. This process also includes imagery related to the environment that this part of you comes from. It can help you to identify subpersonalities from your childhood, from birth, from before birth, and even from past lives.

Here are some tips for success with this process:

- Familiarize yourself with SK and the Soul Centering Process first. You will use these techniques to accomplish the clearing. As an alternative, you can use EFT.

- Isolate a single issue to clear. You will focus on this issue to access a disowned part of yourself.

- Have your journal available, so you can make note of what you discover as you progress.

- Allow whatever comes into your awareness to flow naturally when you prepare to connect with a subpersonality. Doubting your experience during the process will block the flow from the unconscious mind. You can let your rational mind know that it has the option of rejecting the experience later, but not during the process.

- Understand that the goal is to access the fragmented personality as is, not to shift into the state that you want to achieve. People who are new to this type of process sometimes want to go directly to the goal, without completing the healing work. This will come later; first, you have to address the problems this part of yourself is experiencing.

- Aim to be a neutral observer of yourself during the process. This may be difficult at times, but remembering that the fragmented parts of yourself are not your true identity can help. Your true self, your soul, understands how to bring them back into wholeness. The parts are wounded because they feel unloved and abandoned by the soul, so you can begin to help them with love and support.

- Remember that you are in control. All you need to do is to connect with the energy of the issue to complete this process. Additional information increases your awareness, but it is optional; the process does not need to be difficult. If it becomes painful, you can move on to the Reframing and Anchoring or Finger Rolling any time to reduce the emotional intensity.

Now you are ready to make yourself comfortable and begin.

Start by focusing on the issue you want to explore. As it comes into your awareness, let your mind take you to a time when this problem was difficult for you. The issue may be in the present time, the recent past, or your mind may take you to a much earlier time. Whenever it is, focus on your experience at that time. Close your eyes for a moment, and allow the way you felt then to come fully into your awareness.

Now describe how you felt then by writing the thoughts in your journal. The goal here is to bring out all of your thoughts and feelings related to the problem. As you express these feelings, you are connecting more deeply with the part of you who is in conflict. Close your eyes for a moment, and notice how this part of you looks and feels. Ask yourself each of the following questions and write the answers in your journal:

How does this part of you feel physically?
How does he or she feel emotionally?
Does he or she have a name or title?

Ask this wounded part if he or she has a scene from the past that you need to review. If so, close your eyes and look at the scene you find yourself in. Make note of each of the following:

Your surroundings
The clothes you are wearing
Other people around you
What, if anything, is occurring in the scene
How this part of you feels about your possibilities in the world
How he or she feels about him- or herself
The color you would associate with this scene
Any sounds you would associate with this scene

Take the time you need to experience this part and to under-

stand what he or she wants to show you. This is also a good time to write down whatever comes into your awareness, to help you to maintain your focus on this part of yourself. If the experience is painful for you, remember that you are in control. You can fill the scene with loving energy and let the wounded part know that you love him or her. If it is still painful, you can discontinue the experience or distance yourself from the scene physically and emotionally by imagining that you are 50 or 100 feet away.

Before you do the clearing, ask this wounded part if there is anything else you need to know now. And send him or her more of your love, letting him or her know that you are going to help.

Once you have all the information you need, you are ready to use SK. You may also substitute EFT for the Reframing and Anchoring Technique described here. As you continue to focus on the wounded part of yourself, measure the intensity of the experience between one and ten.

Now you can clear the imbalance. Focus again on the wounded part of yourself and place your left hand on your left knee to anchor the experience. Count to ten and release the hand.

Now take a couple of deep breaths, allowing the thoughts of this issue to drift off as you focus on your breathing. With each breath, allow yourself to relax more, so that any tension in your body can melt away and drift gently down into the earth. Notice that even as you continue reading, you can go into a pleasant state of relaxation, guided by your breath.

Now imagine the light of your oversoul above your head and allow the perfect energy to come down from to clear the imbalance you are dealing with. Feel the energy flowing down through the top of your head, permeating your body with its light, then filling all of the space around you. When you feel yourself completely surrounded by this balanced energy, place your right hand on your right knee to anchor the new pattern. Taking another deep breath, feel this energy becoming even stronger, bringing perfect understanding of your issue. As you continue to feel your soul's energy, count to ten and release this hand. If you were not able to connect with the energy of your higher self, focus on a time when you felt strong and good and anchor that energy.

Now allow your mind to clear. Place your right and left hands on both anchors, count to ten, then remove your left hand from your left knee. Count to five while leaving the right hand on the right knee, then release your right hand.

Now take a few nice, deep breaths as your energy shifts. Then focus on the issue again, and see how the wounded part of yourself is doing. Notice how this part of you looks and feels now, compared with how he or she looked and felt before. Measure any emotional intensity you feel now between one and ten.

If there is still some remaining emotional intensity, you can repeat the balancing. Remember that it normally takes a few rounds of R&A to clear an issue completely. As you repeat the process, notice how the subpersonality changes with each round.

When you have finished the Reframing and Anchoring Technique, gently wipe off both anchors. Now notice how the original scene has changed. How does the wounded part feel about him- or herself now? How does he or she feel about his or her possibilities? Notice your emotions and how your body feels. With the expanded awareness of your soul, the experience should be different. Also return to the image of the part that you saw at the beginning of the process. How does this part look now? Notice any changes in expression, clothing, or other aspects of the scene.

If you are still noticing some of the limitations you started with, you can repeat the R&A or return to the process later.

Finally, before completing the process, connect with the energy of your soul in your heart and ask yourself if there is anything else you need to understand about this issue.

Now focus on coming back fully into the present moment. Breathe in active, waking energy. Notice yourself feeling more and more alert with each breath, and come back with a new understanding of yourself and your soul.

Here is an example of the Integration Process. Loren, one of Jane's clients, had recently made some changes in her diet because of health problems. Her doctor had recommended a diet that includes different dietary recommendations for the four blood types. Loren is an O blood type, and the O diet recommends having regular servings of red meat.

Loren is a sensitive person who had been a vegetarian for about six years. By normal standards, she should have been in vibrant health. Instead, she had gained weight and had become unhealthy while on the vegetarian diet. Adding small servings of meat made her feel stronger immediately. She was delighted that the new diet was working, but not about eating animals.

When Loren and Jane started the process, Loren felt tremendous sadness when she focused on eating meat. Connecting on the mental level, she thought that she had no possibilities. This related to her judgment on the spiritual bridge level that since she was such a horrible person for eating meat, she did not deserve anything.

Focusing on the sadness, Loren saw a little girl about eight years old. The child was shy, forlorn, and withdrawn. She was neatly dressed, but pale and thin, as if she had no vitality. The little girl had a bunny with her, who was also weak and sickly.

The intensity of Loren's sadness started at a ten. As they went through the Reframing and Anchoring, Loren's heart was so strongly affected by the sadness that she was unable to make a soul connection, though she had connected with her soul earlier in the session. Instead, Jane had Loren reframe the sadness by thinking of a time when she was happy and strong. After one round of balancing, the sadness was down to a five.

Loren was already feeling better. When she revisited the image of the little girl, she noticed some positive changes. The child looked hesitant instead of withdrawn and felt like she might have some possibilities after all. Encouraged, they repeated the Reframing and Anchoring. Loren still could not run her soul's energy into her heart, but instead of being completely blocked, it now was feeling slushy, which was another positive sign. Jane again instructed Loren to think of a time when she was happy and strong to reframe the sadness.

After the second round, the sadness again was only about half as strong. Loren rated it at two and a half. Now she saw the little girl playing with the rabbit. The child was less pale and the rabbit was healthy; both were signs of further progress. At this point, when Loren focused on the sadness, it shifted to anxiety. She was not sure why she felt anxious, but rated its intensity at five out of ten.

This time, Loren was able to make a soul connection and brought in the light from her soul to reframe the anxiety. After the third round, the anxiety was down to one. Repeating the process brought it down to zero, and Loren felt wonderful. Focusing again on eating meat, Loren understood it as something that she has to do. She could see that it presented an opportunity for her to accept herself no matter what and to make peace with her physical needs.

Loren's story is a wonderful example of the detrimental effect of some foods. We too follow a diet that relates to our blood type, along with our metabolic rates, and have been pleased with the results. We find peace in sending blessings to all of the plants and animals who support our bodies.

ACCESSING SUBPERSONALITIES WITH SK

Figure 8.1 is the Subpersonality Checklist, which you can use to locate wounded inner child personalities, adult personalities, and past life personalities. We recommend familiarizing yourself with the Basic Checklist and the Current Lessons Checklist before using this one, as it is more complex.

To begin, perform the muscle tests in Part One of the checklist to determine if there is a wounded part that needs to be addressed from childhood, from adulthood, or from a past life. If you encounter a part from your childhood, use Part Two to determine the age of the child. On this checklist, a balanced response for all ages is strong. A weak response pinpoints the age when an imbalance occurred. If you encounter a wounded part from your adulthood, use Part Three to determine the age of the adult. In either case, if you come up with more than one age, select one to address now.

By the time you complete Part Two or Three, you may know where the problem lies. If not, you can use the test statements in Part Four to determine if someone you know is connected with the problem. The more clearly you can pinpoint the imbalance, the better are your chances of clearing it completely. A balanced response is strong. A weak response pinpoints a person who was also involved in the incident that created the problem.

Working with past life personalities can be a bit trickier for those who are new to this of experience. Personalities from the time of conception through infancy are similar, because there is generally no conscious memory to help you out. Parts Five and Six provide some suggestions on muscle tests you can perform to find out more about these parts.

Part Five, which pinpoints related issues and emotions, may be useful with past life personalities, as well as with personalities from this life, if you feel that you still need more information after completing Parts Two, Three, and Four. Since past life issues have been with you for your entire life, think about emotions and/or issues that have always troubled you. If you have always had a problem with anger toward authority figures and a fear of heights, for example, you can use muscle testing to determine if these problems are linked with the personality you are exploring. Muscle test questions like "Is this personality linked with my anger toward authority figures?" and "Is this personality linked with my fear of heights?"

With past life personalities, you may also want to use Part Six to determine when and where the past life occurred through a process of elimination. As with personalities from this life, you should address them one at a time if you encounter two or more.

FIGURE 8.1
SUBPERSONALITIES CHECKLIST

PART 1

STATEMENT	STRONG	WEAK
"Do you need to address a wounded inner child?" If so, proceed to Parts 2, 4, and 5.	___	___
"Is there a wounded part of yourself from your adult life who needs attention?" If so, proceed to Parts 3, 4, and 5.	___	___
"Do you need to address a wounded part of yourself from a past life?" If so, proceed to Parts 5 and 6.	___	___

PART 2: INNER CHILD ISSUES

STATEMENT	STRONG	WEAK
"Focus on the time of your conception."	___	___
"Focus on the time from conception to birth."	___	___
"Focus on the time of your birth."	___	___
"Focus on your first year of life."	___	___
"Focus on yourself between age 1 and 5." Use a process of elimination to find the exact age. Exact age: 1___ 2___ 3___ 4___ 5___	___	___
"Focus on yourself between age 6 and 10." Exact age: 6___ 7___ 8___ 9___ 10___	___	___
"Focus on yourself between age 11 and 15." Exact age: 11___ 12___ 13___ 14___ 15___	___	___
"Focus on yourself between age 16 and 20." Exact age: 16___ 17___ 18___ 19___ 20___	___	___

FIGURE 8.1
CONTINUED

PART 3: WOUNDED ADULT ISSUES

Use a process of elimination to determine the exact age.

STATEMENT	STRONG	WEAK
"Focus on yourself between age 20 and 30." Exact age: ___	___	___
"Focus on yourself between age 31 and 40." Exact age: ___	___	___
"Focus on yourself after age 40." Exact age: ___	___	___

PART 4: OTHER PEOPLE ASSOCIATED WITH THE PROBLEM

If, at this point, you do not know where the problem lies, you can identify anyone you relate to it. The goal is to identify who else was involved through a process of elimination. Test the following statements, filling in the age of the subpersonality.

STATEMENT	STRONG	WEAK
"Focus on your mother when you were ___."	___	___
"Focus on your father when you were ___."	___	___
"Focus on your relatives when you were ___." Name of relative involved: _____	___	___
"Focus on authority figures when you were ___." Name of figure involved: _____	___	___
"Focus on your siblings when you were ___." Name of sibling involved: _____	___	___
"Focus on your peers when you were ___." Name of peer involved: _____	___	___
"Focus on _____ (other) when you were ___." Name of other person involved: _____	___	___

FIGURE 8.1
CONTINUED

PART 5: RELATED ISSUES AND EMOTIONS

Fill in the following blank with any emotions or issues that have been troubling you to find out what the subpersonality related to. For example: "Is this personality linked with my inability to lose weight?" or "Is this personality linked with my fear of men?"

STATEMENT	STRONG	WEAK
"Is this personality linked with _____?"	_____	_____
"Is this personality linked with _____?"	_____	_____
"Is this personality linked with _____?"	_____	_____

PART 6: PAST LIFE ISSUES

1. Determine the sex of this past life personality.

STATEMENT	STRONG	WEAK
"Is this part a male?"	_____	_____
"Is this part a female?"	_____	_____

2. Determine the era of this past life personality.

STATEMENT	STRONG	WEAK
"Is this part from the 16th to 20th centuries?"	_____	_____
"Is this part from the 11th to 15th centuries?"	_____	_____
"Is this part from the 1st to 10th centuries?"	_____	_____
"Is this part from before the 1st century?"	_____	_____

Exact century: (use a process of elimination) _____

FIGURE 8.1
CONTINUED

---

3. Determine where this past life personality lived.

STATEMENT	STRONG	WEAK
"Is this part from North America?"	_____	_____
"Is this part from Central or South America?"	_____	_____
"Is this part from Europe?"	_____	_____
"Is this part from Africa?"	_____	_____
"Is this part from Asia?"	_____	_____
"Is this part from Australia?"	_____	_____
"Is this part from _____(other places)?"	_____	_____

Exact place: (use a process of elimination) _____

4. Determine the age of the past life part you need to examine.

STATEMENT	STRONG	WEAK
"Is this part less than one year old?"	_____	_____
"Is this part between age 1 and 5?"	_____	_____
"Is this part between age 6 and 10?"	_____	_____
"Is this part between age 11 and 15?"	_____	_____
"Is this part between age 16 and 20?"	_____	_____
"Is this part between age 21 and 30?"	_____	_____
"Is this part between age 31 and 40?"	_____	_____
"Is this part between age 41 and 50?"	_____	_____
"Is this part older than 50?"	_____	_____

Exact age: (use a process of elimination) _____

Once you have gathered all of the information you need from the checklist, you can use SK to clear any blockages you have encountered. To do this, focus on the information you have gathered about the age, the emotions, and the people connected with the imbalance, and clear the issue with the Reframing and Anchoring Technique. If you feel an urge to find out more, you can use the Integration Process, focusing on the issues or emotions connected with the subpersonality. If you have not determined which emotions apply, just focus on yourself at that time and allow them to surface. This approach usually works, even with issues that started at the time of conception or in a past life.

Here is an example of how powerful this work can be. On the Subpersonality Checklist, Mary tested weak for the time of her conception. As frequently happens, the muscle testing triggered a memory. She told Phillip that as a child she thought that she was a mistake, although she had never dared to discuss it with her parents. When Mary was in her thirties, her mother said, "You weren't a mistake. We just didn't plan you." This remark somehow confirmed her worse fears.

Mary had lifelong issues with rejection that she played out with partners and friends. She was easily hurt, and would worry whether others really cared for her, just as she had worried about whether her parents really cared for her. She wondered if she was lovable and if she deserved to be loved. She believed that "When I care a lot about a person, I am open to rejection. I can love people in general, but I am wary about personal relationships."

As Mary focused on the time of her conception, Phillip did Reframing and Anchoring. The change was dramatic. Now she felt fine about her conception. She also received a message from her soul that she actually was wanted all along. Mary realized she could now feel more compassion toward others, rather than fearing their rejection. "The rejections by others were just reflections of my own lack of self-acceptance."

Mary felt healed. She knew that she deserved to be loved unconditionally, and that she belonged. And, of course, she now tested strong for the time of her conception.

Mary's clearing helped her to connect more with the truth of who she is spiritually, but this may not have been the end of her inner child work. Once you have cleared one age, you may expose another blockage, so you may want to check in with this checklist over time. When Jane started to become aware of the process of healing her inner child, she had a dream that she was baby-sitting for a child who was two years old. One day, she went to see the child. The little girl was angry and did not want to speak with her. Upon waking, Jane recognized that there was a part of her who was two years old who needed attention. Over the next couple of days, she did some clearing work and felt better, but, within a short time, she had a dream about another child who felt ignored and angry with her. This time the child was a little older, around three or four. Jane recognized that she had to take another look.

Clearing inner child issues is primarily the work of the Second, Third, and Fourth Activations, but generally continues all the way through the Seventh Activation. We have also found that different stages of life trigger different aspects of ourselves. In this regard, clearing issues from the past is an ongoing process, where we learn more and more as we mature and reach new levels of understanding.

BECOMING AN EXPRESSION OF THE SOUL

The Integration Process and the Illumination Process, along with the Current Lesson and Subpersonality Checklists, provide invaluable tools that can help you to integrate the disowned parts of yourself and become an expression of your soul. With the Fourth Key, Living Your Divine Purpose, we will focus on the final stages of the journey.

4th Key

LIVING YOUR DIVINE PURPOSE

CHAPTER NINE

Integrating Archetypes

Life is just a mirror,
and what you see out there,
you must first see inside of you.

–*WALLY "FAMOUS" AMOS*

With the personal clearing we experience during the first four stages of the soul's development, we open to a higher awareness of ourselves. We gradually integrate our fragmented parts, so we can live our lives more consciously. In the process, we replace some of the subjectivity and wounding of the ego with the objectivity and wholeness of the soul.

This healing allows ego and the soul move closer to fruitful partnership as we move into the fifth stage and explore archetypes. The first four stages provide height, as we access higher levels of awareness; the last three stages provide breadth, as we integrate the lessons of the archetypes. This helps us to broaden our awareness of ourselves and the structures our society has created to define itself.

THE ARCHETYPAL LEVELS

Our exploration of archetypes begins with Carl Jung's concept of the collective unconscious. Jung believed that the parts of ourselves of which we are consciously aware are just the tip of the iceberg. Below the surface, each of us has a larger personal unconscious, which contains images and patterns of behavior that are unique to us as individuals. We address the personal unconscious in the first four stages. Further down, there is an even more massive collective unconscious, which contains images and patterns of behavior that apply to everyone in a particular culture or, in some cases, to the entire human species. We explore the collective unconscious in the last three stages. Jung felt that it is important to recognize that we are all unique human beings and, at the same time, through the collective unconscious we are all connected to each other and to every aspect of the universe we live in.

Jung called images and patterns that come from the collective unconscious archetypes. Though he was the first to develop this concept in modern times, these archetypal patterns have appeared in the world's cultures through the ages. In fact, Jung first began to explore the collective unconscious by studying how his patients' experiences paralleled ancient myths. By studying mythology, he learned the characteristics of patterns his patients exhibited. This helped him to understand and ultimately cure his patients.

In addition to myths, we can find archetypes in fairy tales, numerology, and oracles like the Tarot, Runes, and I-Ching. We can also explore patterns we commonly find in our society. Our modern versions of mythic characters are our athletes, movie stars, and political leaders. Our lives are surrounded by archetypes that unconsciously influence us on our journeys.

Understanding how these archetypes affect us on different levels is the subject of the Fifth and Sixth Activations. As

Jungian psychotherapist Sukie Colegrave mentioned in her book *Uniting Heaven and Earth,* to the extent the spiritual world of archetypes eludes our consciousness, we are not free, because we are influenced by principles and forces that are beyond our awareness. Exploring the archetypal world is an integral part of our search for the self, which Jung understood to be both unique and universal.

As mentioned earlier, we explore the personal level of the unconscious in the first four activations,. As we bring more and more of our personal unconscious into our awareness, our vision expands. We begin to notice the archetypal patterns that underlie our personal experiences. The Fifth and Sixth Activations involve transcending archetypes that are based on limitation and creating new archetypal patterns that are based on freedom and unconditional love.

The archetypes we explore in these stages exist at progressively broader levels of our society.

- **Personal Archetypes** reveal the roles we play as individuals.

- **Group Archetypes** define our relationships with our friends, families, business associates, and so on.

- **Societal Archetypes** determine how we relate to whole systems and organizations such as large corporations, our local and state governments, religious organizations, and ethnic groups. Beyond these we have large national organizations, including the medical establishment, the banking system, the IRS, the military, the federal government, the FBI, and the CIA, along with our overall national awareness.

Understanding the roles we play as individuals and how the organizations and institutions that make up our society function provide new opportunities. Not only can we experience the soul in our own lives, the soul can begin to manifest its purpose in the evolution of humanity.

PERSONAL ARCHETYPES

The personal archetypes reflect our values and our perspectives on life. Each of us enters a lifetime with gifts to share and lessons to explore. These qualities begin to develop through the roles we play in our families. Depending on a child's programming, he or she may take on the role of the good boy or girl, the failure, the trouble-maker, the whiner, the genius, and so on. A girl's family may expect her to be the most perfect, the prettiest, or the smartest. A boy's family may expect him to be the strongest, the most athletic, or the most powerful.

Many children go along with these expectations and try to emulate the qualities their parents want for them. For the children who are not able or interested in playing this role, their parents may become disappointed, seeing them as bad, stupid, or stubborn. Such children may then take on these identities. As they mature, they carry these identities into adulthood, along with identities related to the lessons and gifts they have come to share. As adults, they play such roles as becoming a success, having a perfect body, caring for others more than oneself, or righting all of the injustices in the world. Each of these roles reflects an archetype.

A major theme in myths and fairy tales is the hero's journey, which represents the spiritual journey to wholeness.

The steps we take on the spiritual journey are described in such ancient systems as the Tarot and Numerology. These esoteric systems illustrate how we move through phases that have specific lessons for us to learn. Over time, we return to the same phases and lessons again and again, each time bringing a higher level of understanding.

Carol S. Pearson, Ph.D., addresses the subject of archetypes in her book *The Hero Within*. Each archetype carries its own perspective, including its unique fears, goals, and understanding of what gives life meaning. Each one sees the world and the behavior of others in relation to this perspective. Based on Pearson's work, we have developed archetypes that correspond to the different levels of our reality. As with all subpersonalities, the archetypes are polarized. For each one we express openly, there is an opposite one we repress. Here are examples of pairs of archetypes that correspond to the seven levels of our multi-dimensional reality:

LEVEL	ACTIVE POLE	PASSIVE POLE	UNIFIED ARCHETYPE
1	Fighter	Weakling	Stabilizer
2	Virile Person	Caretaker	Nurturer
3	Controller	Victim	Manifester
4	Savior	Sinner	Lover
5	Conformer	Rebel	Communicator
6	Wanderer	Destroyer	Visionary
7	Know-It-All	Fool	Sage

Most of us have played the role of one or more of these polarized archetypes at some time in our lives. Through these roles, we focus on the lessons we are here to learn. We have already discussed how our lessons teach us about our divine purpose. The archetypes provide a deeper understanding of how this learning process occurs.

The archetypes are major aspects of who we are. When we learn the lessons of the polarized archetypes, we release their fears and limiting beliefs and integrate their strengths. They transform as we awaken into the unified forms of the archetypes, and free ourselves to embrace our souls. As you read the following descriptions of some personal archetypes, you may be able to recognize aspects of them in yourself, or notice parts that are missing from your experience. Each level starts with the unified archetype, followed by two examples of polarized archetypes. You may also recognize variations or other archetypes that apply to your individual experience.

First Level: Physical Survival

Stabilizer: People playing this role provide stability in the world, understanding that the body is the vehicle of the soul, and that their life energy supports them in whatever they are here to do. However, the distortions of the ego may produce something like one of the following:

- **Fighter (Active):** These people identify strongly with their physical bodies. Body builders frequently play this role. Street gangs also operate from this archetype. They may turn to violence as a way to solve their problems. Their greatest fear is weakness.

- **Weakling (Passive):** This archetype applies to those who cannot gain enough strength to be active in the world. This may take the form of perpetual illness. Their greatest fear is death.

Second Level: Emotions and Sexuality

Nurturer: These people joyfully nurture themselves and others. This includes their friendships, parent-child relationships, and sexual relationships. The nurturer supports all forms of life. However, distortions of the ego may produce something like one of the following:

- **Virile Male or Female (Active):** These people identify themselves with their sexuality. Their greatest fear is lack of sexual prowess.

- **Caretaker (Passive):** These are the self-sacrificing people who give everything for the well-being of others and take nothing for themselves. Their greatest fear is selfishness.

Third Level: Power

Manifester: These people have the energy and drive to get things done. They understand that true power is an inner strength, rather than an outward struggle for control of others. Under the influence of the wounded ego, they may play a role like one of the following:

- **Controller (Active):** This archetype relates well to the business world and the military. Controllers focus on external power, action, and having a strong impact on the world around them. Their greatest fear is losing control.

- **Victim or Martyr (Passive):** This archetype includes people playing roles like the abandoned orphan or the abused wife. As the controllers focus on power and action, victims focus on powerlessness and the suffering of being controlled by others, as they wait for someone to come along and save them, like a damsel-in-distress. Their greatest fear is being exploited.

Fourth Level: Love and Relationships

Lover: These people bring love to their interactions and harmony to relationships. Under the influence of the ego, they may play a role like one of the following:

- **Savior, Critic, or Judge (Active):** These people are determined to stand in judgment and/or save others from their evil ways. A variation on this is the people who believe they need to teach others a thing or two under the assumption that they know right from wrong better than anyone else. Their greatest fear is being judged.

- **Sinner (Passive):** These people succumb to the path of least resistance. By rejecting the concept of having values, they avoid taking responsibility for themselves. Their greatest fear is being held responsible.

Fifth Level: Expression and Creativity

Communicator: These people focus on expressing their souls through art, cooking, music, writing, speaking, and so on. Under the influence of the wounded ego, they may play a role like one of the following:

- **Rebel (Active):** Rebels are determined not to conform, and actively pursue ways to go against the grain of society. Their greatest fear is blending in.

- **Conformer (Passive):** This is the adult version of the good boy and good girl, who behave as those around them would wish. These people are like chameleons that change color to blend in with the environment. Their greatest fear is criticism.

Sixth Level: Vision

Visionary: It is through our vision that we create our reality. With the soul's guidance, the visionary points the way. When this vision is blocked or distorted by the ego, the visionary may play a role like one of the following:

- **Destroyer (Active):** This is the person who destroys everything that has meaning in his or her life. People with strong addictions, like drug abuse or alcoholism, are frequently on a path of self-destruction. They mistake their pictures of reality for truth, without any understanding of how their vision has been distorted by the ego. Their greatest fear is stagnation.

- **Wanderer (Passive):** These people have become so disconnected from their truth that they have no direction in life. They are left wandering aimlessly with no tangible goals. Their greatest fear is commitment.

Seventh Level: Knowledge and Wholeness

Sage: These wise people focus on bringing the soul's wisdom to bear in their reality. Under the influence of the ego, they may play a role like one of the following:

- **Know-It-All (Active):** These people cannot tolerate the opinions of others, because they believe that they already know everything. A variation on this is the Know-Nothing, which applies to those who continuously seek more information, but never feel that they know enough to move forward in life. Their greatest fear is being wrong.

- Fool (Passive): These happy-go-lucky people never seriously try to succeed at anything. Instead, they settle for whatever comes easily. Their greatest fear is boredom.

The archetypes that correspond to the level of your greatest lesson and gift may have a major influence on your life. You may also notice that one of the archetypes applies to your perspective at work, another with your friends, and maybe another with strangers. It is common for different parts to express themselves in different situations. We also play the roles of different archetypes during different stages of life. As each of us matures, we encounter new parts of ourselves to explore.

As the soul becomes stronger and the ego loosens its hold, many people experience an identity crisis. They have released their old ideas of who they are, but have not fully connected with their souls. Interestingly, some people also have a spiritual identity that is no more real than their work identity. If their concept of spirituality is connected to the ego, as with codependent members of spiritual organizations who derive their truth solely from their gurus or leaders, this identity is the same as any other aspect of the wounded ego.

Each of the archetypes has a lesson to teach us as we move forward on the journey to wholeness. In this regard, none of the archetypes are better than the others. The ultimate goal is to integrate the lessons of all of the archetypes. This is how we become complete and free to manifest the soul's purpose.

Figure 9.1 is the Personal Archetypes Checklist, which can help you to determine if you are being limited by any of the polarized archetypes. You may be able to identify them by simply reading the questions. You may also want to use muscle testing to locate them. This checklist uses yes-no responses.

FIGURE 9.1
PERSONAL ARCHETYPES CHECKLIST

STATEMENT	STRONG	WEAK

1st Level: Physical Survival

The Fighter:
"Are you afraid of being weak?"

The Weakling:
"Are you afraid of death?"

2nd Level: Emotions and Sexuality

The Virile Male or Female:
"Are you afraid of lacking sexual prowess?"

The Caretaker:
"Are you afraid of being selfish?"

3rd Level: Power

The Controller:
"Are you afraid of losing control?"

The Victim:
"Are you afraid of being exploited?"

4th Level: Love and Relationships

The Savior:
"Are you afraid of being judged?"

FIGURE 9.1
CONTINUED

STATEMENT	STRONG	WEAK

4th Level: (continued)

The Sinner:
"Are you afraid of being held responsible?"

5th Level: Expression and Creativity

The Rebel:
"Are you afraid of blending in?"

The Conformer:
"Are you afraid of criticism?"

6th Level: Vision

The Destroyer:
"Are you afraid of stagnating?"

The Wanderer:
"Are you afraid of commitment?"

7th Level: Knowledge and Wholeness

The Know-It All:
"Are you afraid of being wrong?"

The Fool:
"Are you afraid of being bored?"

Strong responses to any of the questions on the checklist mean yes and indicate the presence of the polarized archetypes.

You can use the Reframing and Anchoring Technique to clear any blockages you encounter on the Personal Archetypes Checklist. Since the archetypes represent major lessons, you may want to have more awareness of how they have played out in your life. You can do this with the Integration Process or an Integration Meeting, which is described at the end of this chapter. Since there are variations on these archetypes, the part you encounter in the Integration Process or Meeting may not match the exact description provided here. The important thing is to understand the parts of yourself and the roles you play. And, since different archetypes can surface under changing circumstances, you may want to return to this checklist over time.

Another enlightening way to understand the archetypal roles you play is to write the story of your life as a myth or fairy tale. As you write, focus on yourself from the perspective of a neutral observer. This can help you to identify the roles you have played, how they have limited you, and how you have been able to transform them thus far. Writing this story may also provide a direction for more self-exploration.

Here is an example of working with archetypes. Phillip muscle tested Rick for the Personal Archetypes Checklist and found he was unbalanced for the Conformer, who is afraid of criticism. Rick realized there were two aspects of criticism that concerned him. One involved making impulsive comments to others. Rick referred to these as stupid jokes, sometimes made at inappropriate times. He guessed that he did it out of a desire for attention or approval. Each time he ended up feeling guilty and self-conscious, but before long he would find himself doing it again.

Phillip did R&A with Rick, and it reduced the intensity of the problem from ten all the way down to zero in one round. From his soul's perspective, Rick then realized that this joking side was a part of him, and he could accept it without judgment. He now understood that he didn't make lighthearted comments for approval. It was actually a way for him to fit in, which is, of course, the Conformer's goal. He knew he could now bring more awareness to what this part was saying. He also felt he could now accept himself more.

The second aspect of Rick's criticism concerned Gary, his twenty-two-year-old son. Gary had strong religious beliefs; he would proselytize to others and disregard their viewpoints. Rick criticized his son for being narrow-minded, and had many arguments with his son over this issue. Rick felt he was overly critical of his son.

Two rounds of R&A quickly eliminated the self-criticism. Upon reflection, Rick realized that he had needed to tell his son how he felt and that arguing was the only way he could express his concerns at that time. He now felt content with himself and knew that he was doing the best he could.

BALANCING THE MASCULINE AND THE FEMININE

In your soul's development, the Masculine (active) and the Feminine (passive) archetypes are two of the most important parts to explore and integrate. We mentioned these two aspects in Figure 1.3, where we described the two sides of the brain.

The balanced development of the Masculine and Feminine archetypes is an integral part of awakening.

Each of us has both archetypes, but with the domination of masculinity in our society, they can easily become unbalanced by our programming and life experiences. Balancing the Masculine and Feminine archetypes represents a major step on the journey to wholeness.

Many people who are experiencing a spiritual awakening naturally gravitate to activities and places that help them to integrate their masculine and feminine sides. This shift may draw attention from friends and relatives, because the desires of the individual involved can change dramatically. A man who is very knowledgeable and successful in business may suddenly decide to go off to the country and paint pictures. Or a long-time mother and housewife may decide to send the kids to daycare and start her own business. We see such shifts occurring all around us, which is a strong indication of how our society is changing in relation to these archetypes. As a result, the roles we play as males and females also are undergoing a transformation.

With knowledge of subpersonalities, you can contact the Masculine and Feminine archetypes in the Integration Meeting, and find out what each one needs to bring them into wholeness. Their imbalance generally exists at many levels, so it may be an ongoing process that evolves over time, as you reach more and more deeply into yourself.

We have used the Integration Meeting with our students and clients with profound and surprising results. In one such session, Phillip asked a client named Ralph how he felt about the balance of his masculine and feminine sides. Ralph guessed that his feminine side was weak, which they confirmed by muscle testing. He said he had started to strengthen his feminine side, but knew that a lot of restrictions remained. He felt the impact of society's disapproval of men who appeared or acted feminine, knowing that he had internalized society's fears of homosexuality.

As you will see in the description of the Integration Meeting, each part has his or her own chair. When Ralph sat in the seat designated for his feminine side, he pictured a very small camellia flower submerged in water. The flower said that she felt suffocated. Switching to the masculine seat, Ralph saw a brawny, oversized man. This masculine part knew that he was a façade that Ralph puts up for others as a defense mechanism. The Masculine saw his role as one of protecting Ralph from the perceived threats of the world. Moving back to the feminine chair, he noted that the Feminine was afraid that she would not be accepted, because society expects men to act masculine. She felt separate from this superficial masculine world, and longed to expand out beyond the surface. With a basic understanding of both perspectives, Ralph moved to the seat reserved for his soul. As soon as he sat down, he saw a Feminine Spirit. This surprised Ralph; in previous meditations, he had always experienced his soul in a male form. In reality, the soul exists beyond the limitations of gender. The Feminine Spirit explained that she was appearing in a feminine form to show him how to balance his nature and allow him to feel more. Ralph started to see an image of his heart opening, allowing love to flow. The Spirit told him that total acceptance of both sides would allow the Feminine to expand. Moving back to the feminine seat, Ralph saw that the submerged flower had been transformed into a beautiful woman with a radiant smile. She was standing on the sand with her hair blowing freely in the breeze. She hugged Ralph and said, "I love you," weeping with joy.

Ralph again moved to the masculine seat. This part was happy now. Curiously, his masculine side had become smaller. He was less overbearing, but still retained his masculinity. The Masculine welcomed the Feminine. They then merged together, while still keeping their individuality. This merging is a common sign that the integration is complete. To conclude the process, Ralph went back to the Feminine Spirit's chair. She gave the masculine and feminine parts her blessings, and added with a smile, "It's about time."

After this session, Ralph looked much lighter. His heart had opened, allowing more peace to enter. A week later, he dreamed that he was going to have his appendix removed. After the operation, he discovered that he had been cut open all the way up to the neck. He was shocked that the operation was this extensive. Upon reflection, Ralph connected this dream with the Masculine/Feminine Meeting that had opened up much more than he had expected. He felt he was still integrating the profound changes from the process.

THE POLARITIES CHECKLIST

As all of the wounded parts of ourselves are polarized, we can also see the Masculine and Feminine as polarized parts of ourselves that need to be balanced on the spiritual path. There are also other major polarities that you may want to address, which we list along with the Masculine and Feminine in the Polarities Checklist in Figure 9.2. Each set of polarities relates directly to our balanced spiritual development, as well as to balance between different parts of the body. Here are descriptions of each pair:

- **The Masculine and Feminine,** which we have already described, relate to the right and left halves of the body.

- **The Spiritual and Earthly** are important parts to balance on the spiritual path to allow us to move forward spiritually while staying firmly grounded on the physical plane. They correspond to the top and bottom halves of the body.

- **The Inner and Outer** relate to the torso and the limbs. The torso houses the organs, which relate to our inner feelings. The limbs include the arms, which relate to reaching out in the world and the legs, which relate to moving forward in life.

- **The Past and Future** selves relate to the front and back halves of the body. The spiritual path takes us into the present moment, where the past and the future are in balance. Too much focus on either one takes us out of the present moment. If our energy is going into dwelling on things that happened to us in the past or waiting for things to be different in the future, life is passing us by.

FIGURE 9.2
POLARITIES CHECKLIST

Say "Focus on _____," filling in the blank with an item from the checklist.

STATEMENT	STRONG	WEAK
THE MASCULINE AND THE FEMININE		
"... your feminine, receptive side."	____	____
"... your active, masculine side."	____	____
THE SPIRITUAL AND THE EARTHLY		
"... the ethereal, spiritual part of your nature."	____	____
"... the earthly, physical part of your nature."	____	____
THE INNER AND THE OUTER		
"... your private, inner nature."	____	____
"... your public, outer nature."	____	____
THE PAST AND THE FUTURE		
"... your past self."	____	____
"... your future self."	____	____
THE MIND AND THE BODY		
"... the rational, thinking part of your nature."	____	____
"... the physical part of your nature."	____	____

- **The Mind and the Body** polarities deal directly with the tendency so many of us have of "being in our heads." They correspond to the head and the remainder of the body. When we are lost in thought, we cannot be grounded in the body in the present moment. Likewise, if we act without thinking, we are also ungrounded, often making impulsive or illogical decisions.

You can use the Polarities Checklist to determine if any of these polarities need to be balanced. We recommend using the Integration Meeting to work with them, as this will help you to integrate these polarized pairs with the light of the soul and bring the understanding you need to maintain this balance.

Since these polarities are major players on the spiritual journey, you may also want to return to them over time.

THE INTEGRATION MEETING

The Integration Meeting is a variation on the Integration Process, based on a technique called Voice Dialogue, which was developed by Hal Stone, Ph.D. and Sidra Winkelman, Ph.D., and the subject of their book *Embracing Our Selves*. In an Integration Meeting, you can carry on a conversation with several parts of yourself and, with your soul's assistance, reintegrate them. Of course, SK and EFT can help with clearing.

The Integration Meeting is somewhat like acting: you take on roles and become these characters. Each subpersonality has its own seat and you move from one seat to another to speak for the different parts directly. This demonstrates dramatically how real the subpersonalities are. It is also a good technique for just letting go and having fun. The parts can seem to be pretty absurd at times.

Here are some pointers for working with subpersonalities:

- Set aside plenty of time for "getting into your part" and for allowing each part to express him- or herself.

- As with the Integration Process, you want to connect with each subpersonality as is, not as you want it to be.

- Each subpersonality has a distinct appearance, posture, tone of voice and facial expression. Taking on these characteristics can help you to understand the part more fully.

- If you feel uncomfortable with a subpersonality, do not force it. Go on to something else, or clear the emotions you are experiencing with SK or EFT before proceeding further.

- Remain neutral. Parts require impartiality; they need to feel free to express themselves without fear of judgment.

- Parts may change just by bringing them into the open. As always, it helps to bring in the soul for its higher perspective and to assist with resolution.

You will probably find this process easier if you familiarize yourself with the Integration Process first, as this one builds on the skills you develop there. The following instructions relate specifically to balancing the Masculine and Feminine archetypes. Presenting the meeting with these parts provides a structure that people who are new to this type of process can readily understand. Once you are comfortable with it, you can use this process with any of the polarized pairs of archetypes or subpersonalities.

You might want to have your journal handy to document the perceptions of each of the parts. Another option is to speak into a tape recorder. This will allow you to stay connected with the roles you are playing.

Here are the steps in the Integration Meeting:

1. Have at least three seats available. To balance the Masculine and Feminine, you need a chair for the feminine part of yourself, a chair for the masculine part, and a chair for your soul.

2. Start in the chair that is designated for the Soul and do a brief centering process, as you would with kinesiology, to access a neutral and receptive state.

3. Move into the Feminine chair and focus on this part of yourself. She is your receptive, nurturing, intuitive part. Take a few deep breaths and allow your feelings about your receptive, feminine side to surface into your awareness. Then close your eyes and have her describe herself, either out loud or by writing in your journal. Find out if there is a name or a title she would like you to use when addressing her. Then ask yourself how this part of you feels. Following the holistic model we have developed, find out how she feels physically and emotionally, how she feels about her possibilities in the world, and how she feels about herself. As with the Integration Process, make a note of how she looks, what she is wearing, the scene or colors around her, and any sounds that you would associate with this image. Notice especially how your body feels when you take on the role of this subpersonality, and allow yourself to assume the posture of this part of yourself. As you progress, record what she tells you for future reference.

4. When the feminine part has told you everything she wants you to know, get up from your chair, leaving her behind. Look toward the next chair and imagine that the masculine part of you is sitting there. Then, sit down in the Masculine chair and move into this role. He is the active, rational and logical part of you. Take a few deep breaths and focus on how you feel about this part of yourself. Close your eyes and notice how your body feels when you connect with this part of yourself. Take on his posture and notice how it differs from the feminine part. Have him describe himself, either aloud into a recorder or by writing in your journal. Find out if he has a name or title to describe himself and how he feels. Following the holistic model again, find out how he feels physically and emotionally, how he feels about his possibilities in the world,

and how he feels about himself. As with the feminine part, make a note of how he looks, what he is wearing, the scene or colors around him, and any sounds that you would associate with this image.

5. When the masculine part has told you everything he wants you to know, get up from the second chair, leaving him behind. Look toward the last chair and imagine that the Soul or Higher Self is sitting there. Then as you sit down in this chair, move into the awareness of the Soul. Close your eyes and take a couple of deep breaths. Focus on breathing energy into your heart and surrounding yourself with the Soul's energy. As with the other parts, notice how your body feels when you embody this expansive part of yourself. Take on the posture of this part of yourself. Make a note of how he or she looks, what he or she is wearing, the colors around this part, and any sounds that you would associate with this image. Then allow the soul to provide his or her perspective on the status of the Masculine and Feminine, either aloud into a recorder, or by writing in your journal. If the masculine and feminine parts are experiencing difficulties, ask what can be done to bring them into balance and wholeness. Then, from the perspective of your soul, send love to the masculine and feminine parts sitting in the two empty chairs.

6. From here, you can return to the first chair and notice whether the Feminine has changed based on the input of the Soul. Notice if her appearance is different, along with her emotions, beliefs, and how she feels about herself. She may also have more she wants to say in response to the Soul's comments. As an option, you may also want to use SK or EFT to balance any issues she still faces.

7. When the feminine part has finished expressing herself, you can move to the second chair and see if the Masculine has changed based on the input of the Soul and the Feminine. Notice if his appearance has changed, along with his emotions,

beliefs, and how he feels about himself. He may also have more he wants to say in response to the conversation thus far. As an option, you may also want to use SK to balance any issues he still faces.

8. In some cases, this amount of dialogue may be enough to clear any imbalances these two parts of yourself were experiencing. You will know that you are done when each part looks healthy and feels complete. If this is the case, you will generally want to finish with the perspective of the Soul to provide closure to the process. You can do this by moving back to the third chair and asking the Soul for its final comments.

9. If there is still work to be done, continue the dialogue in whatever way is most helpful for re-uniting these parts of yourself. The main purpose of the technique is to speak with the parts and send them loving energy. This alone may change them. With help from the Soul, the parts may be able to return to wholeness and become reintegrated with the soul. Sometimes, however, this may not happen immediately. In such cases, you can return to the process later.

As previously mentioned, you can use the Integration Meeting to unify any archetypes or subpersonalities with the soul. With practice, you can use the process with any part that is having a problem. Start with the part of you who has the problem, your soul, and another interested part. The other interested part generally turns out to be the opposite pole of the subpersonality you started with. This process is a wonderful way to learn more about these parts of yourself.

A client named Theresa came to Phillip to learn more about her fear of expression. In an Integration Meeting, the two parts that her soul mediated were the Scared Girl and the Critic.

While Theresa sat in the first chair, she and Phillip started to discuss her fear. Talking about any issue usually brings that subpersonality to the surface. When Phillip felt that she had connected with her fear of expression, he asked Theresa how this part looked. She described a Scared Girl who was alone in a dark place. She said she was afraid of everything: going anywhere, speaking up, doing something wrong, being laughed at, and being criticized.

As Theresa moved to the next chair, Phillip asked her to connect with another part of herself who was interested in the subject. She accessed the Critic. He was big and mean, holding a pointing stick to correct the girl. He told the Scared Girl to come out in front of people. "It's rude to hide away," he scolded. He added that she could speak up when she wanted to, but she didn't. She would not listen, because she was so afraid. He thought that maybe she was stupid and did not try hard enough.

Having connected with both of the polarized parts, Theresa moved to the Soul's seat. This voice first addressed the Critic. "You are too hard on the Girl. She can only handle so much. She is afraid to try, because she thinks she will fail." Then the Soul addressed the Scared Girl. "If things don't work out, you can try again. Do your best and learn from this. You are not alone; I'm here with you."

Returning to the first chair, the Girl's voice changed as she addressed the Critic. "Knock it off. I'm just a little kid. Your carrying a stick makes me think you will hit me. Stop telling me 'You'll never be able to do it.' Then I never will. Tell me I'm doing it just a little right. I will feel better and try harder. I need your feedback, but if you laugh at me when I make a mistake, I feel humiliated and hide. Then it's easier not to do anything. When you call me stupid, I believe you."

Switching to the second seat, the Critic responded. "I didn't know I was setting such high expectations for you. I thought I was helping you. I am proud of your successes. And thanks for your feedback. I don't really think you're dumb. And I didn't realize I wasn't supportive and that my criticism was so negative for you."

The Girl thanked the Critic and promised to do better next

time. The Soul concluded the discussion advising the girl to go to Theresa (the adult) for assistance. The Girl can now feel free to enjoy herself and relax. She can also benefit from her efforts and learn from her mistakes. The Soul ended by saying, "I love both of you and am here for you."

In this session, the Critic showed how the parts all have positive goals. He actually thought that he was helping, but without the loving guidance of the Soul, his approach was too harsh. Fortunately, as this example shows, once the polarized parts come in contact with the Soul's wisdom, they usually transform quickly. Now, we will explore how these dynamics play out in our interactions with others.

CHAPTER TEN

Developing Spiritual Relationships

Love consists in this,
that two solitudes protect and touch
and greet each other.

–*RAINER MARIA RILKE*

Relationships are the heart of human existence. The people around us provide companionship, entertainment, and inspiration. They may also be targets for our frustrations and anger. Together, we share our challenges and successes and, along the way, others point out our possibilities and our limitations.

The personal archetypes we discussed in the last chapter exist primarily in relation to other people. They are the faces we present to the world. A friend who wants to be liked may play the role of the Conformer. A person who wants others to respect his intelligence could play the Know-It-All. Exploring the personal archetypes sheds new light on our interactions and the group archetypes. Our acquaintances, friendships, romantic relationships, and business relationships bring meaning to our lives, and, where there is conflict, they point to the lessons we need to learn. Each of us has ideas of what a romantic relationship should be, what it means to be a single man or woman, a married man or woman, an employee, a boss, and a friend. As we move forward and grow spiritually, our relationships need to grow with us.

In any given moment, we view those around us either through the fear and fragmentation of the ego or through the love and wholeness of the soul. Figure 10.1, The Seven Levels of Relationships, shows some examples of the differences between the wounded ego's view of our relationships and the soul's view. Our relationships are multi-dimensional, so we need to understand how we are relating to others on all levels.

In our interactions, we synchronously attract experiences to ourselves again and again because of the archetypal roles we play. In considering group archetypes, there are two ways to look at our relationships: the different roles we play and our concepts of different types of relationships.

Here are some examples of group archetypes that correspond the different roles we play:

- Single Person
- Married Person
- Friend
- Mother or Father
- Brother or Sister
- Son or Daughter
- Employee
- Employer
- Business Executive
- Blue Collar Worker
- Boss or Manager
- Spiritual Aspirant

FIGURE 10.1
THE SEVEN LEVELS OF RELATIONSHIPS

LEVEL	EGO	SOUL
General	Experiences co-dependent relationships based on fear and separation	Experiences spiritual relationships based on love, honor, and unity
1. Physical Survival	Sees others as threats to one's safety and security	Sees others as companions in the journey through life
2. Emotions and Sexuality	Relates to others through fear, anger, and other unresolved emotions	Relates to others with joy and a spirit of mutual support
3. Beliefs	Seeks to control and dominate others or to be controlled	Seeks to empower self and others equally
4. Judgments	Exhibits jealousy, judgment, and blame	Accepts and respects others with unconditional love
5. Expression and Creativity	Stifles one's expression and creativity to maintain the status quo	Delights in everyone's unique expression
6. Vision	Regards others as standing between one self and one's goals	Sees others as ways broaden one's perspective, and enrich one's life
7. Knowledge and Wholeness	Focuses on the differences that divide us and keep us apart	Focuses on the spirit that unites us all

Here are some examples of group archetypes that correspond to different categories of relationships:

- Family Relationships
- Business Relationships
- Friendships
- Single Romantic Relationships
- Married Relationships
- How we relate to Strangers

The goal of working with the group archetypes is to understand how we are limiting ourselves with the roles we play, and how we can bring them into alignment with the soul's wholeness. Take the example of a woman who plays the role of the Victim in her romantic relationships. Statistics show that she will tend to go from one abusive relationship to the next until she reclaims her power. Similarly, a man may be fired from one job after another because of his uncooperative attitude until he learns that playing the Rebel is not an effective approach to take as an employee.

The group archetypes also explain why a change in the nature of a relationship often creates conflict between people. A man and a woman who have lived together happily for years may experience a difficult adjustment when they marry. Their relationship is changing from the Single Relationship archetype to the Married Relationship archetype. Everything else may be the same as it was before, but the archetype is different. Similarly, when an employee advances into a management position, his whole personality may change, to the dismay of his fellow workers. In this case, his archetypal concept of being a manager is different from that of being a fellow employee.

Each of our interactions provides an opportunity to move beyond the limitations of the ego through the wisdom of the soul. This takes us from co-dependent relationships to spiritual relationships. Co-dependent relationships are based on the fear of the ego and promote limitation. Spiritual relationships are based on the love of the soul and promote growth and expression. They honor each individual. Here are some characteristics of spiritual relationships:

- They provide mutual support on the soul's journey.

- Each individual is empowered, free from any desire to control others or need to be controlled.

- Each individual exists in sovereignty, free to manifest his or her divine purpose.

Like all of the levels of the soul's development, transcending our limitations and developing spiritual relationships requires awareness and honest self-examination. These relationships are rare now, but they are setting a higher standard for how people will interact in the future.

CO-DEPENDENT RELATIONSHIPS

As with our personal blockages, most relationship patterns are largely formed unconsciously. They are based on rules about how people should behave around each other, along with what they should and should not say and do. The saying "Don't rock the boat" refers to these types of relationships. Everyone involved tacitly agrees to a shared perspective that will not interfere with the group's limiting concepts of reality.

Take the example of a family where the father is an alcoholic. The first rule is that everyone denies that there is a problem. The wife spends most of her energy trying to please her husband, so he will not become upset. The adult son drinks along with his father to fit in with the group, while the adult daughter buys the alcohol to appease her father. They all agree to a limited concept of reality to avoid creating waves.

Viewed energetically, co-dependent relationships create attachments between people. In a Controller-Victim relationship, the Controller's aura may engulf the Victim, much the way a spider spins a web around its prey. There are also webs of energetic cords between people. These are sometimes positive, as with attachments between mothers and the children they nurture. They may also be limiting, as with attachments between a guru and the aspirants whose minds he unconsciously wants to control.

The goal of a spiritual relationship is sovereignty for all concerned. This is also the ultimate lesson of the Fifth Activation. During this stage, each of us is challenged to overcome limitations in our relationships with our families, friends, and associates. With the attainment of sovereignty, each person holds his or her own auric space, free of cords and attachments that create control of, or by, others at any level. This new freedom generally transforms ones concept of relationships.

Psychologically, one goal of awakening is to break all of the unconscious agreements and remove the limitations from our relationships. We strive for relationships that are based on emotions like honor, caring, and honesty.

Spiritual relationships promote our awakening and create unlimited possibilities.

Transforming relationships based on limitation is not always easy; in some cases, it may not even be possible. When you break the unconscious agreements, you rock the boat and are likely to feel the waves. Some of the people in your life may not be ready to change, so some relationships may move into the background or fall away. Fortunately, this shift provides an opportunity for everyone to grow.

THE ROLES WE PLAY WITH OTHERS

To achieve sovereignty, we start by looking at where we are relating to other people through fear, limiting beliefs, and judgments. Examining the archetypes can help us to recognize the roles we play in the various arenas of life. Here are some common archetypes for the roles we play in our society:

GROUP ARCHETYPE	CORRESPONDING PERSONAL ARCHETYPE
Business Executive	Controller
Employee	Conformer
Mother	Caretaker
Father	Know-It-All
Single Person	Virile Male or Female
Blue Collar Worker	Fighter
Spiritual Aspirant	Fool

These archetypes vary from one person to another and from one society to another. Cultural differences explain why there are so many misunderstandings between people from different nations, religious backgrounds, and racial heritages; the unspoken rules are different.

In the United States, a working mother may take on the role of the Controller in her business relationships, the Virile Female in her marriage, the Nurturer to her son, and the Conformer with her friends. Playing these different roles allows her to feel comfortable in each of the situations, but can create confusion when they come together. This is why people can become confused when they encounter people outside of their normal settings, such as when they run into some business associates while they are out shopping with friends. In the case of the working mother, in the moment of that meeting, she somehow needs to reconcile the differences between being a Controller in the eyes of her fellow employees and a Conformer in the eyes of her friends. This may be a difficult, if not impossible, task.

An interesting experiment with the archetypes is taking them into different environments, like taking the Nurturer to work and the Controller into the home. This can teach us new aspects of the archetypes and bring out new parts of ourselves.

Ultimately, as we integrate each of the polarized archetypes with the wisdom of the soul, their limitations are released, allowing us to experience the strengths of the unified archetypes and advance on the journey to wholeness. The Hero ultimately learns that we all are unique, and we all are one.

BALANCING RELATIONSHIP PATTERNS

As we clear our distortions, we change energetically. Our interactions often change, too, because we no longer attract the same energetic patterns to ourselves. There are also times when we may find that we need to move forward without another person if he or she is not able to change. This is frequently the case with abusive relationships. The lesson may be to leave the relationship, whether it is a friendship, a romantic relationship, a family relationship, or a business relationship.

Jane attracted abusive relationships with her employers earlier in her life. Like an abused wife, she would try her best to please them and do everything right. She would usually work harder than most other people and was very productive, but her employers would expect more and more over time. Jane was unconsciously playing the role of the Victim at work. With one particular employer, she finally saw clearly that he treated her differently than everyone else; that she had become the target of his anger and frustration.

One day this employer was reprimanding her for something he thought she had done, when another employee who was listening to the conversation stepped forward and admitted making the error. Jane expected her employer to turn on the other employee. Instead, he paused, then said, "Oh, that's okay," and quietly walked out of the room. In that moment, Jane realized that she was actually attracting his abuse by trying so hard to please him and not standing up for herself. She was just an easy mark. Since there were plenty of other employment opportunities available, she found a more appropriate job and left the abusive employer behind.

Fortunately, Jane did not attract an abusive marriage. We had the good fortune to come together on a spiritual level. We recognized each other as unique individuals and encouraged each other on our journeys. Now that we understand the concept of sovereignty, this is our goal in all of our relationships.

ATTAINING SOVEREIGNTY

Attaining sovereignty is an exciting step. Most people experience a new sense of self, knowing that they do not have to bend to the wishes of others when it is not serving either individual spiritually. In the process, an understanding of the true meaning of a spiritual relationship emerges. Achieving sovereignty is also challenging. We have to look at where our relationships are preventing us from fully expressing the soul's divine purpose. Any person who has control over us may be holding us back.

Being sovereign does not mean that you cannot have a job and work from nine to five. Your profession may be a part of your true purpose, and we all have to live with some rules. The important factor is how other people affect you energetically. When challenged, you need to be able to maintain the strength of your convictions and live your divine purpose.

THE GROUP ARCHETYPES CHECKLIST

Figure 10.2 is the Group Archetypes Checklist, which you can use to find out if there are any group archetypes or specific relationships that you need to examine. As a note, there may be some categories that apply to you that are not on the list, so we suggest considering if there are any other relationships or group archetypes that need to be tested.

When you are in a state of sovereignty, all of the archetypes and relationships on the checklist should all test strong. A

FIGURE 10.2
GROUP ARCHETYPES CHECKLIST

STATEMENT	STRONG	WEAK
"Focus on being single."	_____	_____
"Focus on being married."	_____	_____
"Focus on being a mother or father."	_____	_____
"Focus on being a brother or sister"	_____	_____
"Focus on being a son or daughter."	_____	_____
"Focus on being an employee."	_____	_____
"Focus on being an employer."	_____	_____
"Focus on being a manager."	_____	_____
"Focus on being a spiritual aspirant."	_____	_____
"Focus on (other) _____."	_____	_____

STATEMENT	STRONG	WEAK
"Focus on your mother."	_____	_____
"Focus on your father."	_____	_____
"Focus on your spouse or romantic partner."	_____	_____
"Focus on your siblings."	_____	_____
"Focus on your friends."	_____	_____
"Focus on your business relationships."	_____	_____

If there is more than one of any of the above, focus on each one individually, like different siblings, friends, and so on. Also include any other important relationships, such as adoptive parents or other people involved in your upbringing.

"Focus on (other) _____."	_____	_____
"Focus on (other) _____."	_____	_____

weak response pinpoints an imbalance, which may trigger an awareness of the problem. As with the other checklists, your results using SK or EFT to clear the imbalance will be better if you can be precise about what is out of balance. You may also want to use the Illumination Process or the Integration Process to understand more about what is happening unconsciously. These processes are both effective for focusing on your experience and reframing it with the wisdom of the soul.

Here is an example from one of Phillip's clients. Susan tested strong for her relationship with her employer, but knew she had a problem with the principal at the school where she taught. She did not consider him to be her employer, so she tested strong for that category. She called him her "boss," and when Phillip tested her for that archetype, she tested weak.

Susan felt stress because she didn't feel supported by the principal. He wouldn't look at her when she spoke with him, and he never asked for her input on things that affected her. She said his people skills were poor, and she tried to avoid him. She did, however, want to be appreciated by him.

Phillip asked Susan to focus on her boss and performed the R&A Technique. After anchoring her soul's energy, Susan's outlook shifted noticeably. She calmly said she could respect the principal, in spite of his shortcomings. She could allow him to be who he was, and she was not depending on him to change. She also added with a laugh, "If he doesn't buy into my approach, he can excuse himself. In any event, I know it will work out."

Susan recognized that even though the principal held a position of power and control, his issues did not need to affect her. In merging with her soul, she realized that this relationship taught her about her own strength. She was resourceful and effective, regardless of the circumstances. This challenging relationship was really a self-test. She also understood more deeply the importance of being happy. There is a cost to putting up with negative situations and counting on others for support. She now felt confident about creating positive work situations for herself and those around her.

Here are two more examples from another client. Beth tested weak for being a manager. She related the issue to not wanting to have control over others as her parents and some other people had controlled her. She had never been a manager, but felt that if she did have that role people would look at her with fear and dread. SK eliminated those feelings.

Beth also tested weak for being married. She had recently divorced, feeling trapped and owned in her marriage. She wanted to be on her own and do as she pleased, which she had achieved through the divorce, but she still had some residual trapped feelings from her marriage. SK quickly freed her of these feelings.

Another way to approach this subject is with the Current Lessons Checklist in Figure 6.2. Use the statement "Focus on your relationships (in general or a specific relationship) in relation to _____," going through the levels listed on the form. This will identify the issues more specifically, which may be helpful in some of your close relationships. You can also cross-reference your muscle-test responses with the Seven Levels of Relationships in Figure 10.1. This may help you to understand the qualities you are aiming to integrate at each level. You can then clear any blockages you encounter with SK, EFT, or one of the GTT processes.

CHAPTER ELEVEN

Transcending Society's Fears

The only true hope for civilization –
the conviction of the individual that his inner life
can affect outward events.

—STEPHEN SPENDER

With the Sixth Activation, our attention broadens to the scale of the mass consciousness and the societal archetypes. Bringing awareness to the dynamics of our personal lives and relationships in the Fifth Activation leads us to examine how we fit into the society around us. This is a natural part of the process of fully embracing the power of the soul and connecting with our divine purposes. In the Sixth Activation, we move from the ego's focus on confrontation and competition to the soul's focus on mutual support and cooperation on the societal level. With this awareness, we can see how the same levels of fear and unconsciousness that once pervaded our personal experiences also exist in the organizations that influence whole communities, states, and nations.

M. Scott Peck describes this phenomenon in his book, *A World Waiting To Be Born*. He notes that organizations avoid confronting difficult issues just as individuals do. As a result, large amounts of unconscious activity exist throughout society, in the operations of businesses, religious organizations, and departments of the government. And, as you might have guessed, organizations play the same roles that individuals do. Many of our governmental institutions, like the military and the IRS, play the role of the Controller. Many religious institutions play the role of the Savior. Different cultures may play the role of the Conformer or the Victim. It can be illuminating to think about how we interact at the societal level.

Unfortunately, most people do not recognize how deeply entrenched they are in the structures of the mass consciousness that control our entire society. We have now come full circle. As mentioned earlier, people operating within the limits of the mass consciousness are largely unable to think for themselves or take responsibility for their actions. They rely on the cultural consensus to determine what is right and wrong, and what has value. What they miss is how that consensus has been built on the fears of the ego and, in the case of our society, on the desire for material gain instead of inner fulfillment.

Our society is oriented almost exclusively toward the material aspects of life. Many people are like mice running on a treadmill, constantly rushing about out of fear of losing the trappings of success. They do not recognize the possibility of stopping and taking an honest look at the world that we have all created.

BALANCING SOCIETAL ARCHETYPES

Fortunately, healing at this stage does not involve changing the entire mass consciousness. This is not possible. Instead, it involves understanding how you are limited by society's fears so that you can be free to express your soul's purpose. Most people are in fear of the power of institutions like the IRS or those who write their paychecks. You do not need to change these systems to be free. You simply need to be free of their emotional control. By the way, this does not free you from paying taxes or obeying the law.

The societal archetypes include:

- Monetary System
- Educational System
- Medical System
- Taxation System
- Banking System
- Political System
- Media
- Military
- City, State, and Federal Governments
- Organized Religions
- Organized Professions like Physicians and Attorneys
- Labor Unions
- Cultural Groups like Nations and Races
- CIA
- FBI

As we move into a new century, the challenge we face as a society is to bring the same love and honor we seek within ourselves into the structures that turn the wheels of all of humanity. As more and more people move into the wisdom of the soul, our society will change. This is already happening as people come forward with new ideas for interacting in the workplace, with government agencies, and so on.

The Internal Revenue System has recently been the subject of media attention for using illegal tactics, threats, and lies in their dealings with the public. They also were shown to have a practice of targeting people who lack the resources to fight back. Fortunately, this practice has come into the light through the willingness of some brave individuals who decided not to be silenced by fear. While a single individual cannot change the IRS or the medical establishment, the changes each individual makes do affect those around him.

In *A World Waiting to be Born,* M. Scott Peck describes civility as consciously motivated behavior. "To become more civil, humans must become ever more conscious of themselves, of others, and of the organizations that relate them together." This consciousness, in turn, leads to personal liberation. As you examine the list of societal archetypes, you may come to understand that your soul's purpose is connected with making changes within one or more of these systems.

If you are a teacher, as Phillip is, your divine purpose may include helping to bring more awareness the educational system. If you are in the medical field or in the field of alternative medicine, your soul may be here to help with the transformation of the medical system. As you progress through the stages, your growing awareness creates a beacon of light that helps others to recognize their unconscious patterns. And, regardless of your purpose in life, your immediate goal is personal liberation, to exist within society without being limited by it.

THE CORNERSTONES OF A SOUL-ORIENTED SOCIETY

The four cornerstones of a soul-oriented society provide some ideas of where we are heading both individually and collectively. They correspond to the higher forms of expression that are possible for us all:

1. **Creative Expression:** Transform life based on mere survival into one based on the unique expression of each individual.

2. **Joyful Existence:** Release all fears, unresolved emotions, and lack of support.

3. **Cooperation:** Replace competition with cooperation so that all individuals may freely manifest their divine purposes.

4. **Honor:** Transform judgment into acceptance and honor of all forms of life.

As more of us move toward the wholeness of our soul, the organizations and institutions that run our society will follow suit and find outlets for the soul's expression. The fear we see in our institutions is simply a reflection of our own inner worlds, and the possibility of genuine change is in our hands.

THE SOCIETAL ARCHETYPES CHECKLIST

Figure 11.1 is the Societal Archetypes Checklist, which you can use to locate any archetypes that are out of balance at this level. Where you are balanced, you should get a strong muscle response while focusing on each of the societal archetypes. A weak muscle response indicates imbalance.

It is interesting that rules of etiquette recommend avoiding discussions on such subjects as money, politics, and religion. This is because most people are not able to deal consciously with these issues, so conversations can easily become ugly. We can address them most effectively when we have completed our work at the individual and group levels. Until we have reached this point, attempts to balance the societal archetypes may not be completely effective.

If you still have a lot of inner child issues, personal issues, or relationship issues, you may want to save this checklist for another time. Although SK will generally balance almost any issue temporarily, you need to be ready to work at the societal level for the effects to be lasting. As with other issues, it helps to be specific when you do the balancing. While you may have some success with focusing on the IRS and doing Reframing and Anchoring, the process will be more effective if you focus on a specific time when you were disturbed by the IRS and use R&A on the emotions you experienced at that time.

Here are some examples of clearing societal archetypes. Hal tested weak for the educational system. He traced this response

---

FIGURE 11.1
SOCIETAL ARCHETYPES CHECKLIST

STATEMENT	STRONG	WEAK
"Focus on money."	_____	_____
"Focus on the taxation system."	_____	_____
"Focus on the medical system."	_____	_____
"Focus on the political system."	_____	_____
"Focus on the educational system."	_____	_____
"Focus on the legal system."	_____	_____
"Focus on labor unions."	_____	_____
"Focus on the military."	_____	_____
"Focus on organizations like the FBI and CIA."	_____	_____
"Focus on your church or spiritual activities."	_____	_____
"Focus on your local government."	_____	_____
"Focus on the state government."	_____	_____
"Focus on the national government."	_____	_____
"Focus on cultural groups like nations and races."	_____	_____

You may be able to think of a few of your own, like large companies and governmental organizations with which you interact.

	STRONG	WEAK
"Focus on _____."	_____	_____
"Focus on _____."	_____	_____
"Focus on _____."	_____	_____

---

to how his son Ted passed the first four grades of school without ever learning to read. Ted had cheated on tests, copying answers that he couldn't understand. R&A quickly cleared Hal's uneasiness. He realized that the teachers were not at fault; they had over thirty students in a class. He now felt that he could accept the educational system in spite of its faults.

Hal also tested weak for labor unions. He had accepted the role of president of his AFL-CIO, because no one else in the union was willing to oversee the upcoming wage negotiations. He felt annoyed with the elected officials who engaged in trivial discussions and argued over insignificant matters. After Phillip did SK with Hal, his perspective changed immediately. He felt calm, and the negative feelings were completely gone. He could accept the union and realized that the meetings served a function, even though the trivia consumed some time.

Another client named Mary tested weak for the Legal System, which she associated with her mother, who had been in and out of prison for drug use since Mary was a young child. Though the intensity of the problem was a nine, it vanished after just one round of SK. Mary then realized that her mother's legal problems did not have to affect her. After all, she could not control her mother's actions. Because of this short process, Mary felt freer to live her own life.

These examples show how quickly and powerfully you can make changes with SK. When addressing a particularly intense issue related to one of the societal archetypes, you may want to use the Unification Process or the Integration Process to connect with the part of yourself who is having the problem.

YOUR FAMILY HERITAGE

Another part of the Sixth Activation is clearing limitations related to your family heritage. Most of us are unaware of the limiting beliefs our families have instilled in us that come from their religious, cultural, racial, or national heritage. On a positive side, our ethnic heritage is like the spice that gives a dish its unique flavor. On the negative side, our heritage can limit the soul's expression.

People from different races, religious groups, and countries interact from different archetypes. Members of a whole cultural group may characteristically play the role of the Victim, the Controller, or the Rebel. With this in mind, it is easy to understand why there are so many misunderstandings and conflicts in the world. Conversely, when we recognize the patterns and the diversity of life, we can bring more understanding to our interactions and more easily pinpoint how we can take the next step on our journey.

An individual's cultural heritage may produce different kinds of limitations. Some cultures identify with suffering, blocking the possibility of experiencing joy and playfulness. Some identify with a need to hoard valuables that blocks the free flow of resources. Collecting old unused things may block the possibility of receiving something new and more meaningful. Some identify with antiquated codes of honor that stifle their individual expression. At this stage, you may want to review your family relationships and look for traces of these kinds of limitations. Figure 11.2 is the Family Heritage Checklist, which you can use to locate blockages related to your family heritage. These issues are generally deep and usually warrant the use of one of the deeper GTT processes.

Here is an example from a session with Jane and Ruth. Ruth wanted to deal with issues relating to her sexuality, which she also noticed in the other members of her family. She did not need a checklist to know that the problem was related to both sides of her family. In addition to having a background of alcoholism on both sides, she recognized that all of the members of her direct family, which included her mother, father, and sister, had issues related to sexual abuse. Because of these issues, Ruth believed that sex had to be furtive to be exciting. The men she was attracted to reminded her of her father and her sexual relationships left her feeling violated.

Interestingly, Ruth and Jane started the session by working with another seemingly minor problem, which turned out to be connected to this core issue. Ruth was feeling overwhelmed by the piles of paper that her husband Jeff left all over the house. She had tried to speak with him about cleaning up after himself, because the clutter was disturbing her, but he refused. She was angry that he did not acknowledge her feelings.

Ruth's anger started at an eight. After one round of Reframing and Anchoring with her soul's energy, it was down to zero, but sadness immediately came up in its place. The sadness was at a six. Now she felt pain in her heart, because Jeff did not care enough to consider her feelings. She could see that his lack of consideration was creating the same sense of being violated that she had wanted to address earlier.

In the second round of Reframing and Anchoring, Ruth was no longer able to open her heart to receive her soul's energy, so Jane had her focus on a time when she felt strong and good. After the second round, the sadness was completely gone.

Jane thought that this would be a good time to use the Heart Focus. When asked what her heart looked like, Ruth said that it was like a cave. The cave represented a warm and safe place to withdraw from other people, where she would not

---

FIGURE 11.2
FAMILY HERITAGE CHECKLIST

STATEMENT	STRONG	WEAK
"Focus on your mother's family lineage."	___	___
"Focus on your father's family lineage."	___	___
"Focus on your brother or sister."	___	___
"Focus on your spouse or partner's lineage."	___	___

be violated. This image brought up the feeling that she needed to withdraw to avoid allowing the men in her life to take her energy. She felt that as long as she was available, they would take more and more. In addition to feeling violated, Ruth felt overpowered and dishonored. Believing that she could not withdraw physically, she would withdraw into her imagination to offset these feelings.

Now Ruth was at the core of the issue. Her feelings of being violated were at a ten. She again focused on a time when she felt happy and strong as they did the R&A. In the process, her feelings of being violated shrunk down to nothing.

To check their progress, Jane returned to the paper issue and asked Ruth how that felt now. Ruth had some minor irritation, which she rated at a two. This time her heart was open, so they did another round of R&A, bringing in her soul's wisdom. When they were done, the cave image had transformed itself into an inviting earth home. In Ruth's mind, an earth home was a symbol of nurturing. While a cave was dark with no life in it, the earth home was covered with green, and there was sun everywhere. While a cave was for hibernating, the earth home was for sharing; people were welcome to come in.

COMPLETING THE SIXTH ACTIVATION

Completion of the Sixth Activation represents a large step in your awakening. At this point you have largely risen above the limitations of the third dimension. This achievement is generally accompanied by an infusion of understanding that can take some time to integrate. Once this process is complete, however, you find a new inner strength that will provide stability as you prepare to fulfill your divine purpose, which is the focus of the Seventh Activation and the next chapter.

CHAPTER TWELVE

A New World Dawns

When through one man a little more love and goodness,
a little more light and truth comes to the world,
then the man's life has had meaning.

—ALFRED DELP

With the completion of the Sixth Activation, you prepare to freely express your divine purpose. The Seventh Activation is when you get to the bottom of any remaining issues, to move into nearly full consciousness, leaving just enough space in the unconscious mind to allow you to integrate your ongoing experiences. As you release the remaining limitations, your higher senses open more.

In this stage, you integrate the overview of our third dimensional reality, how we have limited ourselves, and what we can potentially achieve if we release the blockages that hold us down as a society. In your awakening process, you have moved outside of the limitations of the mass consciousness. With the Seventh Activation and Transcendence, you build the energetic strength you need to exist within the mass consciousness without being adversely affected by it. You can be in the world, but not of the world. This allows you to participate in society in a role that will further your purpose and help others.

YOUR ROLE IN SOCIETY

Humanity needs people in all parts of society who are living consciously. Being a transformational healer may be one person's purpose. Another person may be a waiter in a restaurant who infuses the food with light and shares loving energy with those who come to dine. Another person may work for a government agency, where she helps those around her to look at life from a higher perspective.

The environment you are in becomes the vehicle through which you express your purpose. The thing that distinguishes people who have achieved transcendence is not what they do or where they live. It is their internal state. Wherever awakened people are, positive changes occur.

The evolutionary process is mysterious, but we sense that as more individuals reach this level of awareness, humanity as a whole will have an opportunity to transcend the limitations of our current reality. Larry Dossey, M.D., describes the potential of connecting with the soul in this way in his thought-provoking book *Recovering the Soul*:

> If the caretaking of the soul has been thought in the past to be solely an exercise of the individual concerned about his personal fate, this may no longer be the case. Today it is the fate of the Earth, not just of single persons, that is also our concern. Can the recovery of the individual soul help in the rescue or preservation of our imperiled planet? Perhaps.

Like Dossey, many people see attaining this level of awareness as a necessity for the survival of the planet. We will not find the solutions to the problems we face collectively as long as we are in limitation. It is interesting how complex our problems seem when viewed through the lens of fear, and how simple they seem when viewed through the lens of love. Imagine the potential humanity would have if everyone lived in a state of unconditional love. Focus for a moment on your heart and open to the loving energy of the soul that you hold there. Now imagine a world where all of the people are in this state. On such a planet, there could be no war. There could be no hunger. The inhabitants could not intentionally cause harm to other species or to the planet itself. This is where the potential for transformational change exists.

As long as there are individuals who are selfishly motivated by fear and greed, we will continue to face problems like inequality, hunger, pollution, and destruction. No amount of legislation is going to solve our problems, because they are here as lessons for us to learn from. Synchronously, even the pollution that clouds the air may be seen as a reflection of the blockages that cloud our awareness. We will discover a way to eliminate it when we are clear within ourselves.

By this stage in your journey, you are not affected very much by what is happening in the mass consciousness. You have achieved energetic sovereignty on all levels and have a strong connection with your soul to guide you. You are nearing the achievement of complete freedom.

The ultimate goal is co-creation, which involves understanding how your role and your actions relate to the good of the whole in each moment.

Reaching for this goal, you prepare to transcend third dimensional existence, based on physical survival and fear, to a higher level of reality based on creative expression and love.

Until an individual reaches Transcendence, the cellular fear of death is the body's motivation for living at the physical level. In the Seventh Activation, we actually see a point of transition where the individual can release this fear and shift into a life based on the desire for creative expression. This transition is only possible when the ability to co-create and to become an expression of the soul is strong enough to replace fear as the prime motivating force for sustaining life on a physical level. Such expression requires a high degree of energetic integrity.

THE FREEDOM TO CO-CREATE

The Seventh Activation is where the rubber meets the road. Where the Sixth Activation brings an infusion of understanding, in this final stage, it is time to make the soul's expression a reality. You need to uncover any remaining imbalances to reach your goal of co-creation. With clients who are working at this level, we generally find another layer of blockages that need to be released and old habits that need to be changed to allow them to express themselves freely. This clearing gives the soul complete freedom to co-create in each moment, without inner limitations or the control of others.

As mentioned previously, the goal here is not perfection. Completing this activation does not mean that you will be totally free of such emotions as fear and anger. Instead, it means that you will be able to integrate the difficulties you encounter with greater ease and return quickly to a balanced state. By this stage, you will have cleared most issues related to your inner child, your relationships, the archetypal levels, and your family heritage. Nonetheless, new situations may bring up issues that have not surfaced before. Fortunately, SK, EFT, and GTT provide the tools you need to clear most issues and move forward again.

To complete this activation, you need to have a good understanding of your soul's purpose. The best way to bring this purpose to fruition is to write down where you are aiming to go. If you have not done so already, you may want to do it now. We have personally found that we need a strong sense of direction to propel us forward coupled with an open mind to allow for possible changes. Reviewing the enormous shifts we have personally experienced during the last decade, it is obvious that ten years ago we could not have known how dramatically different our lives would be now. Nonetheless, we can now look back and see how each step we took led to the next and gradually transformed our reality. Now we focus more on the next step and allow the more distant future to become clear over time.

We had an experience with a client named Virginia who had reached this stage, but got stuck. We suggested several times that she write down what brings her the most joy, but encountered resistance. Virginia finally realized that there must be something she needed to examine. She recalled that as a child her parents had thwarted her desires so regularly that she gave up on the idea that she could have anything she really wanted. The mere mention of writing down her goals brought a strong negative reaction. Once Virginia recognized what was occurring, however, she was able to release the blockage and move forward again toward living her divine purpose.

In addition to being free to express one's divine purpose in each moment, co-creating involves taking full responsibility for oneself and one's actions. Caroline Myss, Ph.D., describes the goal of co-creation in her book *Anatomy of the Spirit*. "As spiritual adults we accept responsibility for co-creating our lives and our health. Co-creation is in fact the essence of spiritual adulthood: it is the exercise of choice and the acceptance of our responsibility for those choices."

REVISITING THE CONTINUUMS OF CHANGE

Now we will review the Continuums of Change we introduced in Chapter One. By the time you reach the Seventh Activation, you have traveled light years on your journey to awakening, and each of the continuums provides a way to measure your progress. Even those who have not reached this stage can benefit from reviewing these continuums. Wherever you are, these descriptions may trigger an awareness of imbalances you need to address. To review each continuum from the perspective of the Seventh Activation:

- **Relationship with the Soul:** With the completion of the Seventh Activation, the soul is firmly in charge. The ego has returned to its rightful position as an intermediary between the multi-dimensional reality of the soul and the practical requirements of living in the third dimension. Now the soul's guiding light shines onto all that we do.

- **Energy Field:** The aura has been transformed. The darkness is largely gone and the aura has expanded tremendously in size. The light of the soul shines brightly from within. A person who has completed the Seventh Activation holds a transformational frequency that helps others to move forward on their spiritual journeys.

- **Awareness:** The mind has changed from being largely unconscious to largely conscious, with a small amount of space in the unconscious mind to allow for integrating one's ongoing experiences. The individual has a strong connection with the soul, accompanied by an understanding of his or her motivations.

- **Love:** Judgment has been largely removed, opening the heart to unconditional love, which is food for the soul.

- **Relationships:** Interactions with others have shifted from codependence to sovereignty. The aura is largely free of energetic cords and attachments to others.

- **Power:** Genuine inner strength and power have replaced the need to have power over others or to allow others to have power over oneself.

- **Conscience:** The individual has moved from a state of irresponsibility to taking full responsibility for his or her actions.

- **Feelings:** The individual is largely aware of his or her emotional state, along with the feelings of others.

- **Dependability:** Awareness of one's feelings coupled with a willingness to be personally responsible allows us to be emotionally reliable. In this state, we are not subject to causing harm to ourselves or those around us. This is an important factor in our ability to co-create with the divine plan, because we cannot help others if we are subject to doing harm.

- **Truth:** The subjective truth of the ego has been replaced by the objective truth of the soul. Disagreement is largely replaced by understanding, which unifies us on a common path.

- **Trust:** Fear of harm has been replaced by trust in the universe or trust in God that everything will work out in accordance with the divine plan or a higher purpose. This sense of trust is accompanied by an awareness of how synchronicity is continuously at play and, as a result, all is well.

- **Will:** Indecision and the resulting inability to follow through on a course of action have been replaced by a strong sense of direction that is linked with fulfilling one's soul's purpose in all aspects of one's life. This spiritual will is coupled with a willingness to surrender one's personal will to that of God or a higher power, which provides comfort when the results of one's efforts are not what one expected.

The development of these qualities also relates to the transformation the energy field undergoes on the journey.

ANOTHER LOOK AT THE ENERGY FIELD

We have described how the energy field gradually expands and embraces more of the soul's light as we awaken. As with any healing process we experience along the way, the aura builds light and stability from the inside out. If you look at the Seven

Spiritual Activations in relation to the Seven Levels of Healing, each activation focuses on creating stability in one of the levels, starting with the etheric and working outward to the higher mental level. We are actually experiencing expansion on all levels with each healing process and each activation, but each stage emphasizes growth on one level.

Activating the seven levels of the energy field is similar to filling a seven-shelf bookcase with books. If you try to fill the top shelf first, the bookcase will fall over, because it lacks stability on the lower shelves. Instead, you fill it from the bottom up. Of course, you can start adding books on the upper shelves before the lower shelves are completely full; in our spiritual development, we are actually expanding on all levels while maintaining a specific focus on one level during each stage. Since we continue to expand and grow, none of the shelves are ever completely full, but we add to each one in a way that keeps the whole bookcase in balance.

It is just amazing how everything within us is connected and how there is a divine order to our spiritual awakening. Here is a description of the Seven Spiritual Activations, with a correlation to the Seven Levels of Healing.

- The First Activation, Recognition, provides the groundwork we need to integrate the soul's energy in our physical reality. The first level of healing relates to our physical well-being.

- The Second Activation, Renunciation, creates stability on the emotional level as we learn to rely on ourselves more for emotional support. The second level of healing relates to our emotions and sexuality.

- The Third Activation, Empowerment, involves gaining a new perspective on our possibilities and a taste of genuine power. The third level of healing relates to the power of our beliefs and attitudes about ourselves.

- The Fourth Activation, Embracing, relates to embracing the wounded parts of ourselves who have become disconnected from the soul. The fourth level of healing relates to love.

- The Fifth Activation, Sovereignty, relates to archetypes and how we express ourselves in the world. The fifth level of healing relates to our expression and creativity.

- The Sixth Activation, Integration, completes the picture of our reality with the societal archetypes. The sixth level of healing relates to our vision.

- The Seventh Activation, Transcendence, releases us from the limitations of the physical plane and moves us into co-creation, which involves integrating the light and wisdom of the soul into our physical reality. The seventh level of healing relates to wisdom and wholeness.

As we become increasingly stable on the spiritual path, we also embrace more positive qualities, which we describe on the Transcendence Checklist.

THE TRANSCENDENCE CHECKLIST

Figure 12.1 is the Transcendence Checklist, which defines positive qualities and emotional states to strive for in this stage. This checklist includes items from the Continuums of Change in Figure 1.1, the Current Lessons Checklist in Figure 6.2, and the Seven Levels of Healing in Figure 7.2. As you approach wholeness, you should test strong for each of these items. Where you test weak, there is more work to be done.

As with the archetypes, your ability to balance the items on this checklist corresponds to your degree of preparation. If you have cleared most of the issues in the earlier stages, you will be more likely to get lasting results from clearing at this level. Regardless, going through this list may provide insight about where to look next.

If you test weak for any of the items on this checklist, ask yourself "What is stopping me from _____?" We have found that this question can bring awareness to what is occurring. This alone may provide enough information for you to proceed with some clearing work. Those who are familiar with *Getting Thru to Your Emotions with EFT* may also want to use the Levels of Psychological Reversal provided there to pinpoint the problem. This may trigger more understanding and also provides a basis for clearing with EFT or SK.

The Transcendence Checklist can also be the starting point for using the Illumination Process or the Integration Process, if you are not certain what is in your way. This process will help you to bring more awareness to what is occurring, so you can clear any blockages you encounter with SK or EFT.

As mentioned earlier, clearing is most effective when it is specific. If you are aware of having a lot of blockages relating to the earlier activations, clearing at this level may be too general to have a lasting effect. It is most useful for clearing the final traces of blockages on the continuums as you approach Transcendence. Regardless, testing for the statements in Figure 12.1 can provide insight into where you need to look next.

Here is an example of a session with Jane and Judy, who was focusing on completing the Seventh Activation. She was following her spiritual path, but felt that something was missing. To locate the blockages, Jane started by performing kinesiology on Judy using the Transcendence Checklist. Judy tested weak for creating her soul's true desire, honoring her truth, experiencing joy, feeling supported, her inner vision, and having genuine freedom. When Jane asked her which one felt the strongest, Judy said that it was feeling supported.

Jane and Judy decided to use the Illumination Process to heal the blockages. Focusing on the emotional level, Judy was afraid that she would not be successful. Focusing on the fear brought up concerns about her abilities (mental level) and about being intelligent enough (spiritual level). She also felt pain and sadness about not being in a relationship.

FIGURE 12.1
TRANSCENDENCE CHECKLIST

STATEMENT	STRONG	WEAK
"Focus on creating your soul's true desires."	____	____
"Focus on owning your genuine power."	____	____
"Focus on honoring your truth."	____	____
"Focus on honoring the truth of others."	____	____
"Focus on a life of self-expression."	____	____
"Focus on experiencing joy."	____	____
"Focus on experiencing unconditional love."	____	____
"Focus on taking responsibility for yourself."	____	____
"Focus on trust and feeling supported."	____	____
"Focus on your inner vision or intuition."	____	____
"Focus on having the will to follow through."	____	____
"Focus on having genuine freedom."	____	____
"Focus on experiencing peace."	____	____
"Focus on wholeness and unity."	____	____

You may think of some other positive qualities to strive for.

"Focus on _____ (other)."	____	____
"Focus on _____ (other)."	____	____
"Focus on _____ (other)."	____	____

Judy felt that fear was the strongest emotion, at around seven out of ten. Viewing the issue as a landscape, she saw a barren scene, with sand and hills. The wind was making indentations in the sand, which Judy found pretty in their own way, but noticed the absence of greenery and people. The only living things she could find were some insects in the sand.

They did R&A, bringing in Judy's soul energy to reframe. After just one round, the fear was down to a one. Reviewing the landscape, Judy first only saw shades of color in blue and indigo. She also felt like she had risen way up above the scene. Jane asked if she could fly down closer, so she did. Now Judy saw plants swaying in the wind that looked like reeds with green tips. The sand was still there, but as she looked at it, it changed into blue water, and the plants flowed with the movement of the water. Judy sensed that the water was a perfect temperature and that she was a part of it. She could also see that there was a bottom, which provided support.

With the fear still at a one, Judy sensed that there was still some separation and that she should also be able to sense herself as part of the plants. They repeated the Reframing and Anchoring, which completed the clearing. (Note that you could also use Finger Rolling here.) Now Judy saw shades of blue and gold. The leaves on the plants were broader with beautiful blossoms at the base of each stem. She now saw a school of fish swimming around and felt a force in the water that was bringing everything together. All of the colors in the landscape were merging, and the fear was gone. Judy felt like she was at the center of creation and that everything was coming together.

This process was quite profound for Judy. She could feel herself integrating the energetic changes as she spoke. When they were done, Jane asked Judy how she was feeling about not being in a relationship. Judy felt some sadness of being alone, which she rated at three out of ten in intensity. Jane asked her to see these feelings as a landscape. Judy saw a desert scene with low purple mountains. The scene was not totally dry.

There was sagebrush in bloom, a bit of snow on the mountain-tops, and a blue sky with wispy clouds.

Rather than repeating the R&A, Jane asked Judy to bring down her soul's energy. The soul is, after all, the most powerful healer, and Jane knew that Judy could achieve a strong connection. As she focused on embracing the soul's light, Judy saw the sun's rays coming down and felt good and warm. She understood that being herself was the most important thing, and she now felt supported in what she was guided to do. A silvery blue lake appeared in the landscape, along with some birds and prairie dogs.

Now that the clearing was completed, they went back to the muscle testing and Judy tested strong for the entire list. This was a good example of how things are related. An imbalance in one area may also show up in other areas. Likewise, clearing one issue may have a positive effect on other issues.

NOURISHING YOUR SOUL

How you treat yourself and conduct the activities of your life can also affect your ability to live your divine purpose. Many people on the spiritual path experience a desire to be more aware of their needs on all levels. It is never too early to start finding ways to fill these needs. Figure 12.2 covers The Seven Levels of Care.

Nourishing yourself with love and honor generally requires some awareness and commitment to changing habits that do not support your soul's expression.

Your feelings on this subject may make a good entry for your journal, as you review how you relate to each of the Seven Levels of Care.

Physically, you need to honor and care for your body, so that it can serve the soul. You also want to create a home environment that resonates with your frequency. Depending on where your soul's purpose leads you, you may even be able to select your geographical location. Some people feel best near the ocean, in the mountains, or in the desert. Towns, cities, states, and nations also hold unique frequencies. You can probably think of places that energize you, as well as places that feel draining. Being in a location that is disharmonious with your frequency places a burden on your energy system.

In a similar way, stores, restaurants, businesses, and institutions are all infused with the collective energy that created them. A restaurant that operates from a love for food and a desire to share this pleasure with others has a positive energy; a restaurant that operates solely for profit, where the employees are treated without respect and the food is prepared without love has a different energy. We recognize this collective energy in what we describe as good vibes or bad vibes in different environments. We may not know what we are perceiving, but we know when the energy is positive, nurturing, and loving or, conversely, negative and fearful. Of course, living your purpose may include being in a specific place. If you find yourself in an area that is less than ideal for your frequency, you can still create a positive home environment.

It is only because of the limitations of the third dimension that we believe we cannot meet all of our needs. It may take some time to make adjustments, but if you set your course for the direction in which you want to go, you will get there. Beyond the physical level, each of us also has emotional, mental, and spiritual needs. Emotionally, we can create a joyfully nurturing environment for ourselves and others; mentally, we can open to the unlimited possibilities that we all have; spiritually, we can cultivate the genuine spiritual relationships that provide support and companionship on the journey. On the higher spiritual levels, we can find outlets for our expression and creativity, exercise our intuitive abilities and connect with the truth of who we are as magnificent spiritual beings.

FIGURE 12.2
THE SEVEN LEVELS OF CARE

LEVEL	LESSON	LEVEL OF CARE
1	Physical Survival	Having adequate rest and a suitable place to live
2	Emotions and Sexuality	Creating a joyful and nurturing environment for both yourself and those around you
3	Power	Opening to free thinking and unlimited possibilities
4	Love and Relationships	Cultivating spiritual relationships based on honor and unconditional love for yourself and others
5	Expression and Creativity	Promoting a life based on creativity and the expression of your truth
6	Vision	Exercising your ability to visualize and create according to your soul's purpose
7	Knowledge and Wholeness	Cultivating and following your inner knowing and guidance

Filling these needs brings joy, as does the company of others who are like-minded. Even those who have reached the Seventh Activation are usually holding onto old habits that do not serve their awakening. We all need to look at old ways of being that do not fit into a creative, spiritual life. This is something that you can do at any time, wherever you are on the journey. Nurturing and cultivating yourself with the Seven Levels of Care provides fertile ground for the soul's emergence. In *Handbook for the Soul*, editor and contributor Richard Carlson discusses nourishing the soul:

> Our connectedness to our Soul is critical to our ability to feel peace and love, to act in kindness toward others, and to feel a sense of gratitude and wonder for life. To nourish the soul means to attend to and care for the parts of ourselves that make us happy and enable us to become kinder, gentler, more compassionate, and loving. As we get into the habit of nourishing the Soul, we move to an entirely different level of life.

THE FREQUENCY OF CO-CREATION

The changes we see in the energy fields of individuals who have integrated the frequency of co-creation are awe-inspiring. The energy field is largely stable and the soul's light flows through all of the levels of the field, guiding the individual. The ego has largely transformed into the true personality, which now seeks to assist the soul. This stability and inner light represent the completion of Transcendence.

We are just starting to see what happens next. Once the energy field has stabilized in the frequency of co-creation, it transmits rays of light into the universe that represent all of the things the individual is aiming to co-create. Each ray is a color that resonates with the specific nature of the co-creation. They are quite beautiful. From this new configuration, we can also see that the completion of the Seventh Activation is not the end. Instead, it opens another doorway into the unknown.

PAVING THE PATH TO THE FUTURE

Those of us who are awakening at this time are paving the way for many more to follow. As the months and years pass, we have noticed that it is becoming increasingly easier for people to complete each of the activations. The road is still pretty rocky, but each individual who moves boldly forward clears the spiritual path a bit more.

Every step you take on your individual path is also a step for humanity.

As your individual light brightens, you light the way for others to follow and prepare the path for all of humanity to rise into a new way of being. The rocky road you travel down today will someday be more like a freeway, and you will watch in awe as those who now linger behind move rapidly forward to meet you further down the road.

So now your soul's purpose is tied closely with the journey of all of humanity. This emphasizes the importance of moving beyond the influence of those who would hold you back. This book provides material that you can return to over time to help you on the way. We believe that amazing healing tools like SK and EFT are becoming readily available to allow us all to move easily along on our spiritual paths. In so doing, we are building the road to tomorrow, removing the rocks and smoothing the way for ourselves and others.

Those of us who choose to align our lives with our souls' true purposes are in the position of influencing this transition by creating joy, love, and freedom in all aspects of our lives. When enough people reach this point of awakening, the frequency of the mass consciousness as a whole will raise humanity into a higher dimension of reality. From there, we will have an opportunity to connect with even higher frequencies, and possibilities that go beyond the range of our imaginations.

Exploring Your Dreams

In the examples in this book, we have shown how our dreams provide another road map of our journey through life and our spiritual awakening. They show us where we have been, where we are stuck, and where we are going. This appendix provides some background information on dreams, along with descriptions of the techniques we use to understand them.

When the conscious mind lets go and we sleep at night, our unconscious mind is far from inactive. This is the time when the unconscious mind, along with the soul, processes information from our daytime activities. Our dreams give us messages about how things are going and what we need to address in our lives. When we are consciously striving to change unproductive unconscious patterns, the messages hidden in our dreams become especially important.

TYPES OF DREAMS

In an attempt to simplify, the rational mind may want to create a single definition for the significance of the images and characters in our dreams. This is not possible because each of us processes information in a unique way, and we all experience different types of dreams that serve a variety of purposes. Some dreams vent emotions we stifled during the day; others bring significant symbolic messages about the direction of our life; still others aim to tell us something about our health. To begin, we need to explore some of the types of dreams:

- **Associative Dreams:** Some dreams are related to sensations in the environment, like the sound of sirens, the sensation of heat, the itching sensation of a mosquito bite, and so on. Any experience of the five senses can create an associative dream.

- **Literal Dreams:** Dreams sometimes serve to process daily activities, like a difficult situation at work. In these cases, the dream characters and images may just be who and what they are in our waking lives.

- **Symbolic Dreams:** These dreams contain symbolic images and messages from the unconscious. We have to interpret the meanings of these images to understand the messages in the dream. The characters in symbolic dreams are usually aspects of ourselves, who may appear in the form of a person we know in our waking life. For instance, a mother in a dream may be the mother part of the dreamer.

- **Spiritual Dreams:** These are very special symbolic dreams that provide messages from our souls. They can be recognized by their beauty and clarity.

- **Pre-Cognitive Dreams:** These are dreams that may be trying to tell us something about the future.

- **Recurring Dreams:** These are usually symbolic dreams we have over and over that are telling us that we need to work through something. The same dream may recur over a period of weeks, months, or years. Once we get the message, they stop.

- **Nightmares:** These are often symbolic dreams, too, which are related to our fears. They may also have literal meanings related to a past life or event.

- **Lucid Dreams:** These are special dreams where the dreamer is able to participate consciously in the dream. With most people this occurs rarely, if ever.

UNDERSTANDING DREAM IMAGERY

In working with dream imagery and personalities, we are focusing on symbolic and spiritual dreams, which also includes some recurring dreams and nightmares. To understand the symbolism, we use variations on the processes we have already presented in this book.

From our experience, interpreting dreams is easier than some people think. You do not have to spend hours writing down all of the things a symbol might mean or pouring through books on imagery. In fact, since each person's internal communication system is unique, the interpretations you find in books may not relate at all to the message your unconscious mind and your soul want to convey.

For example, Jane once had a dream that there were red fire engines driving through the town where she lived. In a book on symbolism, she read that this means there is an emergency she needs to be aware of. Her own dream interpretation, however, revealed that the fire engines actually meant that she was protected and safe. This interpretation related much more closely to the way the fire engines felt in the dream, very peaceful and steady, rather than harried and out-of-control.

Jane related the red color of the fire engines to her base chakra, which is about physical well-being. Their symbolic presence in her life was positive and made her feel secure. This color can have many other meanings, however. Red may be related to anger or an infection in the body. The important thing is what feels right to you in relation to the dream.

Regardless, the most effective way to find out what is occurring in a dream is to connect directly with the parts of yourself who are involved. Here are the methods we use:

- **Soulful Interpretation:** One of the simplest methods is to go into a Soul Centering Process, review the dream in your mind, then ask yourself in this centered state what an image from the dream or a part of the dream means. Since the rational mind is likely to interfere with the interpretation as it enters your awareness, have your journal ready, and write down whatever comes into your mind. When you have the interpretation for one image or part of the dream, go on to more until you understand the whole dream.

- **Exploring Dream Characters and Images:** You can speak with the characters in a dream just like subpersonalities. This can be done by doing a variation on an Integration Meeting and speaking with one or more of the characters in the dream. You may want to start with soul centering, then imagine the chairs in your mind. You may only need two chairs, one for you and one for the dream figure, or as many as you have characters in the dream. Ask the dream character to come in and speak with you. Notice how it looks, how it feels emotionally, and so on, just as you would in an Integration Meeting. This technique may also be extended to speak with images in the dream, like a tree, a road, and so on. We just ask them what they what they represent and what they want us to know.

- **Dream Enhancement:** This technique is useful when you feel that you have remembered part of a dream, but something is missing. In a soul-centered state, you may first wish to begin with the characters and images that you remember, then allow the story to continue like a movie to reveal its entire meaning. This can be done much like exploring a past life or inner child experience with the Integration Process.

How to Muscle test

This appendix is an edited excerpt from our book *Getting Thru to Your Emotions with EFT*. For more information on using muscle testing with EFT, refer to that work.

You can use kinesiology alone or with another person. We will describe ways to do both. Receiving accurate results requires focused awareness, some practice, and an ability to be neutral about the results. Both the provider and receiver need to be open to the information that is coming up from the unconscious without drawing any premature conclusions about the results.

THE CENTERING PROCESS

Before starting with kinesiology and any other healing work, we use a short relaxation process to center ourselves, along with our clients and students. This brings all involved into a state of balance that facilitates the healing process. Energetically, we normally see a lot of static around people, which comes from all of the energy they are exposed to throughout the day. Removing the static clears up the picture and facilitates the deeper healing work. Doing this process before muscle testing also brings you into a state of presence where you feel neutral and open to whatever the body may reveal.

We suggest something like the following script, which you can read slowly aloud or to yourself. It is most effective if you can close your eyes occasionally and focus your attention on your body. If you are reading the process to yourself, you may want to pause between sentences and close your eyes. Allow yourself to feel what is happening in your body, and to imagine the ball of energy that surrounds you and flows through you.

Take a few deep breaths. Imagine that you are inhaling clear, fresh air, and as you exhale that you are releasing any tension you are holding in your body. As you continue to focus on your breath, imagine that you are firmly grounded with a cord that extends from the base of your spine to the center of the earth and that you are surrounded by a ball of energy. Focus on releasing with each exhale. Allow any tension you feel in your body to melt down the grounding cord and into the earth, where it can be easily absorbed, so you feel more relaxed with each breath.

Now imagine that the ball of energy around you extends at least a few feet on all sides – above you, below you, to both sides, to the front and in the back – so that you are completely surrounded and protected by it. Now ask any energy that is not your own to move out of this ball. We all pick up energetic debris as we go through our daily lives, just like a table top picks up dust. If you ask this energetic debris to leave, it will. Just take in a couple more breaths of that clear energy, and feel the debris drifting away, back to its source.

When this is done, ask to return all of your own energy to you. Just as we pick up energy from other people and places, we leave bits of our own energy wherever we go. Now you want to feel this energy returning to you, allowing you to feel whole and complete.

Now focus for a moment on bringing clear energy into your mind with each inhale, so it feels clear, balanced, and alert. Feel this clear energy moving into both sides of your brain, so that your mind is balanced and so that any left-over thoughts from the day can drift off for now. Allow yourself to be here in this moment with a clear mind.

When you feel clear and relaxed, take another deep breath, bringing in clear focus to help you with the kinesiology.

ARM TESTING WITH TWO PEOPLE

When you are centered, you are ready to start muscle testing. One of the easiest ways to use kinesiology is with a partner. We suggest the following arm testing method:

1. **Position the Person to be Tested:** Have the person to be tested, whom we will call the receiver, stand erect, holding one arm out straight to the side. The elbow and hand should be extended, so they form a straight line that is parallel with the floor, with the palm of the hand facing down. Either arm may be used for the testing, as long as it is in healthy condition. You should not perform this type of muscle testing on an area of the body with an injury.

2. **Position the Person Performing the Testing:** The person who is to perform the testing, the provider, then stands either in front of or behind the receiver, facing the extended arm. The provider places one hand on the receiver's shoulder for stability and the other hand on top of the extended arm, at the wrist, so the provider's hand is touching the wrist lightly, but not exerting any pressure. Placing the hand on the wrist before starting the testing allows the receiver to become accustomed to the touch.

3. **Review the Testing Procedure:** To test, the provider says a phrase for the receiver to repeat aloud, starting with "My name is _____." When the receiver has completed the statement, the provider pushes straight down on the extended arm, at the wrist. Here are a few tips.

- Allow the receiver to complete the statement and push on the arm itself, not on the hand. If you push on the hand, you are actually testing the wrist, which is generally not strong enough for this type of test.

- To be sure the receiver is paying attention, say "resist" just before exerting pressure on the arm.

- Hold the hand that will be pushing flat, and push straight down with the palm, gradually increasing the pressure to test the resistance.

- Avoid any jerky or chopping movements or gripping on the receiver's arm.

4. **Test for accuracy:** The first few tests should be designed to determine the strength of the receiver's arm and the accuracy of the results. Start with the receiver's name, then test for another name and a few other easy questions, like the date and the location you are in. A true statement should generate a strong response and a false statement should generate a weak response. In addition to testing the accuracy of the results, the first few questions provide base data on the difference between a positive and negative response.

   If the receiver does not provide accurate results to the first few tests, do not proceed further until you have corrected the problem. There are a few considerations:

   - The receiver may be dehydrated. Have him or her drink at least a full glass of water. Retest and proceed if the results are accurate.

   - The receiver may not be centered and grounded. Repeat the Centering Process to bring him or her back into the present moment. Retest and proceed if the results are accurate.

If you are new to muscle testing, it is generally easiest to start with a partner and practice arm testing until you feel competent. Then you can move on to self-testing.

SELF-TESTING

Self-testing has some benefits. The most obvious is that you do not need to have another person around. As you develop your skills with muscle testing, you may also find it easier to test yourself, even when there is another person available. When you have developed your skills in muscle testing, the main reason to test other people is to demonstrate their bodies' responses. With practice, you can get the same information testing on yourself, even if you are testing for another person. This is called surrogate muscle testing.

The One-Hand Method

There are several ways to perform self-testing. We prefer the One-Hand Method, because it leaves the other hand free if you want to test a substance. Another advantage to this approach is its subtlety. You can do this without drawing attention to yourself, so you can use it anywhere. We use this form of muscle testing extensively in our consulting work to pinpoint the source of a problem, to determine which procedure to use next, and so on. Here is the technique we use:

1. Hold one hand with the middle finger extended straight out from the hand. We generally recommend using your non-dominant hand, because this leaves your dominant hand free to hold a substance you want to test, if desired.

2. With this method of self-testing, the middle finger serves the same purpose as the extended arm in arm testing, and the index finger corresponds to the hand of the provider who is exerting pressure on the arm. Hold the index finger over the middle finger, touching lightly.

3. Proceed with questions just as you would with arm testing, re-

sisting with the middle finger and exerting pressure with the end of the index finger. You can confirm the reliability of your results by testing a series of questions to which you know the answers and testing the responses you receive.

As a note: some people prefer to use the index finger as the extended arm and the middle finger to exert pressure. You can experiment with both and decide if either one feels comfortable to you. If not, your may prefer using two hands.

The Two-Hand Method

This is one of a number of ways to muscle test with two hands.

1. Hold the first hand out, and form a loop with your thumb and index finger. This hand will be the equivalent to the extended arm. You can use either hand, but may prefer your non-dominant hand. With this method, you will test your ability to hold the thumb and finger of the first hand together.

2. Hold the thumb and index finger of your second hand together, and extend the fingers so that you can place them inside of the loop you have formed with the thumb and finger of the first hand. The thumb of the second hand should be touching the thumb of the first hand, and the index finger should be touching the index finger of the first hand.

3. Proceed with questions just as you would with arm testing, resisting with the thumb and finger loop while you try to pull the loop apart with the thumb and finger of your second hand.

INTERPRETING YOUR RESULTS

Once you have completed the testing, you need to interpret the results. You are drawing information from the unconscious mind and the body's innate intelligence, so the results may not match the receiver's conscious intent, thoughts, or desires. A strong response to a question indicates that the statement is true to the receiver or that the condition described is understood as beneficial in the mind of the receiver. A weak response indicates that the statement is untrue to the receiver or that the condition described is not understood as beneficial to the receiver.

The statements that draw a strong response show what we are attracting to ourselves. So if a person tests strong for anxiety and weak for money, he may not be able to create the kind of life he wants. This is why kinesiology is so powerful. It is a way to find out what you are attracting to yourself.

TIPS FOR SUCCESS AND ACCURACY

Small changes in technique can produce big changes in the results you get using kinesiology. As we have mentioned, successful use of kinesiology generally requires practice. The following suggestions may also help you to increase your effectiveness with kinesiology.

1. **Use test statements to confirm accuracy.** Always start with some test statements to be sure the receiver is responding well. Start with his or her name. Then test other simple statements, like the city you are in, the current year, etc. If you are not able to get accurate responses to these questions, we do not recommend proceeding further with testing.

2. **Be sure the receiver is ready.** Always finish the statement you are testing before applying pressure and be sure the receiver is resisting. Say the statement, like "Your name is Joe." Then say "resist" just before pushing to be sure the receiver is resisting.

3. **If in doubt, repeat the test.** If there is any doubt about whether the receiver was distracted or whether the result was strong or weak, repeat the test.

4. **Be sure the receiver is not pushing upward.** The receiver should be resisting the downward pressure, not pushing upward. Pushing upward involves other muscles and will interfere with the accuracy of the results.

5. **Communicate with the receiver.** The receiver may know where the problem lies or experience a sudden recognition about the source of the problem. When you get significant test results, ask if the receiver understands what they mean.

6. **Keep the ego out of the way.** Muscle testing is not a contest. Any kind of competitive battle, where the provider and/or the receiver are trying to prove something, will interfere with the results. Being neutral about the results is the keys to successful muscle testing for both the provider and the receiver.

7. **Relax and take your time.** Test responses are sometimes confusing, so it is important not to rush yourself. You may have to stop and think for a moment to be sure that you understand what the result of a test means.

The *Getting Thru to Your Soul, Part 1* video shows how to use kinesiology. Refer to Appendix D for more information.

The Short EFT Sequence

This appendix is an edited excerpt from our book *Getting Thru to Your Emotions with EFT*. For more information, refer to that work.

The Short Sequence is the starting point for using EFT. Once you identify the pattern you want to release, it takes less than a minute to complete. There is a summary of the steps in this process in Figure C.1 and the locations of the tapping points in Figure C.2.

We will break down the steps in the procedure here, because there are some subtleties that can affect your success.

STEP 1: THE SETUP

To begin, it is important to understand that EFT works with specific emotions. While you may receive results over time applying EFT to a general subject like self-image, it is best to be specific. The setup identifies an emotion to clear. Similarly, using EFT on physical symptoms may be more effective if you can identify the related emotion(s). You can also try using

---

FIGURE C.1
THE SHORT SEQUENCE

---

1. **THE SETUP:** Focus on bringing an emotion or issue into your awareness in the present moment. The key to the success of this process is to feel the emotion and set up the disruption in the meridian system.

2. **THE EVALUATION:** When you have brought the emotion up to its full intensity (or whatever intensity feels comfortable), measure how strong it feels between one and ten.

3. **THE AFFIRMATION:** While rubbing the "Sore Spot" on the chest (see the diagram in Figure C.2 for location) in a circular fashion, repeat the following affirmation three times: "Even though I have this _____, I deeply and completely accept myself."

   Note: If you cannot rub the "Sore Spot", you can tap continuously on the "Karate Chop Spot" instead, while repeating the affirmation.

4. **THE TAPPING SEQUENCE:** Using your index and middle fingers, tap with a medium pressure about seven times on each of acupuncture points in the order shown on the diagram while repeating the following reminder phrase once at each point: "This _____."
   Note: You can tap on the points on either side. It doesn't matter which you use.

5. **THE RE-EVALUATION:** When you have completed the tapping sequence, take a moment to focus on the emotion or issue again, and notice how it feels. Evaluate it again between one and ten to bring any difference in your experience into your awareness.

FIGURE C.2
TAPPING POINTS FOR THE SHORT SEQUENCE

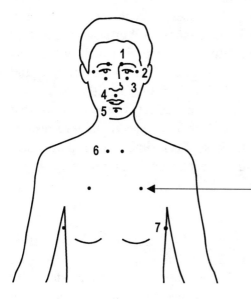

1. Eyebrow

2. Side of the Eye

3. Under the Eye

4. Under the Nose

5. Chin (just below the fold)

6. Collarbone

 SORE SPOT

7. Under the Arm (tender area about 4" below the arm pit)

EFT with the physical symptoms. This sometimes works. If not, you can take your healing process to a deeper level with the GTT processes in this book.

Aspects

With any emotional pattern, there are one or more feelings or aspects. In a case like fear from a dog biting you at the age of four, there may be only one aspect, and one round of the process may completely clear the blockage. This is often true for phobic responses, which may be the result of a single highly traumatic experience. In other cases, there may be a number of aspects associated with a single emotion. For example, a child who was belittled by his father over a period of 10 years may have 100 aspects that are associated with the anger, fear, and resentment he has carried with him into adulthood. If each round of the process removes one aspect, you may think that he will need to do the procedure 100 times to achieve results. Fortunately, this is not the case. Each time you do the process, you clear one aspect, and the rest become less intense.

Multiple Emotions

From our experience, most patterns clear completely within about one to six rounds. An emotion may also change after doing one or two rounds. For example a person may start with sadness and, after a round or two, experience anger. This means that anger is another aspect of the problem that was hidden under the sadness. With each round, you need to review the quality of the emotion and determine if it is actually the same one you felt before.

You may also start with more than one emotion related to a single problem. In this case, decide which one is strongest, and start there. If none is strongest, just start anywhere.

One of the best things about using EFT is that it is gentle.

If an emotion is painful, you do not have to bring it up to its highest intensity to be successful. You may intentionally separate yourself from the emotion by imagining that there is a veil between it and you, or by imagining that the emotion is a distance away from you.

STEP 2: THE EVALUATION

Before you start tapping, you have to measure the intensity of the emotion between one and ten, where one is the lowest intensity imaginable and ten is the highest. The goal is to bring the intensity down to zero, where there is no remaining trace of the feeling. You need to quantify how strong the emotion is in the present moment, not the intensity you experienced last week or last year, or the intensity you imagine you might experience some time in the future. As a note, you can measure the intensity of physical symptoms in a similar way.

If you cannot even guess the intensity, or if you are dealing with something you cannot quantify, don't let that stop you. Just make note of how you feel, so you can compare it to how you feel after you finish the procedure. Your ability to identify the intensity will improve over time.

STEP 3: THE AFFIRMATION

This step addresses any unconscious blockages that may prevent you from achieving results with EFT. This phenomenon is known among users of EFT as Psychological Reversal (PR). You eliminate PR by repeating an affirmation that releases judgments and limiting beliefs. The developers of EFT estimate that psychological reversal is only present about 40 percent of the time. But, using the complete overhaul principle, they include a generalized affirmation in the Short Sequence that clears most forms of PR.

The affirmation is "Even though I have this _____, I

deeply and completely accept myself." You fill in the blank with the specific emotion or problem you are aiming to clear. So you would say something like: "Even though I have this anger, I deeply and completely accept myself," or "Even though I have this fear of public speaking, I deeply and completely accept myself." For a physical problem, you can say something like "Even though I have this headache, I deeply and completely accept myself."

Repeat this statement aloud three times aloud with conviction, while rubbing continuously on the Sore Spot on your chest, which is shown in Figure C.2. You can locate this spot by starting at the collarbone, then moving your fingers down past the first rib a few inches from the center of the chest. If you have a medical reason for not rubbing on the Sore Spot, you can tap continuously on the Karate Chop Spot instead. It is located on the side of the hand below the little finger, right around the middle of the fleshy part of the hand.

STEP 4: THE TAPPING SEQUENCE

Start the tapping sequence immediately after completing the affirmation. Hold the index finger and middle finger of one hand together and tap approximately seven times with the ends of these fingers on the points shown in Figure C.2 in the order shown and described below.

As you tap on each point, you repeat a reminder phrase one time aloud. Repeating the reminder phrase helps you to stay focused on the issue you want to clear and sends a continuing message of your intent to your unconscious mind. The reminder phrase is "This _____," filling in the blank with the same name you used in the blank for the affirmation. If the affirmation was "Even though I have this grief, I deeply and completely accept myself," the reminder phrase is "This grief." You simply say "This grief" as you tap approximately seven times, repeating it once at each point.

For the points that are on both sides of the body, you can tap on either side. You need to tap hard enough to send some energy through the meridians, but the tapping should not be painful.

The tapping points are acupuncture points, so they are generally tender to the touch. This sensitivity should help you to locate the points. Here are the locations of the points.

1. **Eyebrow:** At the inside edge of the eyebrow, above the inside corner of the eye.

2. **Side of the Eye:** Next to the outside of the eye, on the temple.

3. **Under the Eye:** Just below the middle of the eye, near the edge of the bone.

4. **Under the Nose:** In the indentation just between the middle of the nose and the middle of the upper lip.

5. **Chin:** On the middle of the chin, just below the crease.

6. **Collarbone:** On a tender area close to the end of the collarbone, next to the u-shaped indentation below the neck, just under the bone.

7. **Under the Arm:** In the tender area on the side of the chest about four inches below the armpit.

STEP 5: THE RE-EVALUATION

When you finish the tapping, take a nice, deep breath, and allow the energy to settle for a moment.

Once you feel settled, you are ready to re-evaluate. Return to focusing on the original emotion or issue, as you did before. Measure the intensity between zero and ten, and compare it with the original intensity. In most cases, there is a significant difference. The emotion may be completely gone. If not, the important thing to note is the difference. It generally takes more than one round of the process to release an emotion completely. These are the possibilities to consider:

1. **Partial Relief:** The intensity of the emotion is lower than when you started, but it is still above a two in intensity. Repeat the Short Sequence to clear the remaining emotions.

2. **Complete Relief:** The intensity is gone completely. In this case, focus on being in a situation you are likely to experience in the future that would previously have triggered the emotion or issue to see if you get any emotional intensity. If you do, repeat the Short Sequence to clear the remaining intensity. If not, the pattern may be completely gone.

3. **Little or No Relief:** The emotional intensity has not changed, or you have completed several rounds and the intensity has not changed much. When this happens, we recommend using the Complete Sequence, which is described in our EFT book or one of the techniques in this book.

There is no way of knowing whether an emotion will return or not. If it does, you can simply repeat the process.

REPEATING THE SHORT SEQUENCE

If you have achieved partial relief with the Short Sequence, you are ready to repeat the process. As you evaluate the intensity of the emotion or issue again in Step 2, notice if it is the same or if it has shifted to another emotion or issue. Physical symptoms may even move around in the body. This is positive. It means that they are releasing.

If what you are experiencing has changed, you can work on the new issue in the same way as the original one. If you do not notice any difference in the quality of the emotion other than intensity, you can repeat the procedure with the same emotion. In this case, you need to distinguish it from the disruption you cleared in the first round by calling it something slightly different like "This remaining _____." If you said, "This fear" the first time, call it "This remaining fear" the second time. When you repeat the affirmation, say something like "Even though I still have some of this _____, I deeply and completely accept myself," or "Even though I have this remaining _____, I deeply and completely accept myself."

The reminder phrase will be "This remaining _____." Each time you repeat the process with the same emotion, you need to change the label slightly to identify that you are addressing another the aspect.

.

Resources

SPIRITUAL KINESOLOGY VIDEO TAPES AND AUDIO TAPES

Getting Thru to Your Soul: Video Tapes.

These three tapes offer step-by-step instructions on how to do all the techniques in the book. Seeing the processes in action will help with your timing, precision, and presentation. Using real examples and demonstrations, the videotapes show examples of common problems. The procedures have commentaries by Phillip and Jane Mountrose.

- **Tape One:** Spiritual Kinesiology & the Basic Techniques.

- **Tape Two:** Inner Child, Relationships, and the Advanced Techniques.

- **Tape Three:** Archetypes, Subpersonalities, and More Advanced Techniques.

Getting Thru to Your Soul : Two Audio Tapes.

This two-tape set provides guided versions of the GTT processes from this book, with background music. They will help connect and deepen your relationship with your soul. These tapes allow you to sit back and relax, while we guide you through each of the processes.

INTUITIVE DEVELOPMENT AUDIO TAPE PROGRAM

We present the techniques on audio cassette tapes that allow you to experiment with each one as you listen. The tapes are accompanied by a short manual that outlines the program.

OTHER TAPES FROM HOLISTIC COMMUNICATIONS

Getting Thru to Your Emotions with EFT: Video Tapes.
These two tapes present the processes described in our book *Getting Thru to Your Emotions with EFT* through real examples and demonstrations. Seeing the techniques in action will help with your timing, precision, and presentation. The videotapes offer examples of common problems that are different from those covered in the book. The procedures have commentaries by Phillip and Jane Mountrose.

- **Tape One** presents the EFT processes.
- **Tape Two** presents the GTT processes.

Getting Thru to Your Emotions with EFT : Two Audio Tapes.
This two-tape set provides guided versions of the GTT processes presented in this book, with background music. These tapes allow you to sit back and relax, while we guide you through each of the processes.

Getting Thru to Kids: The Five Steps to Problem-Solving with Children Ages 6 to 18: Two Audio Tapes.
This audio set gives you the essence of Phillip Mountrose's award-winning book, read by the author. Uplifting and easy-to-follow, great for deepening your communication skills.

Tips and Tools for Getting Thru Kids: 25 Great Ways to Communicate with Children and Teenagers: **Two Audio Tapes.** This audiobook includes all 25 easy-to-use tools from the award-winning book. Read by the author.

OTHER BOOKS FROM HOLISTIC COMMUNICATIONS

Getting Thru to Your Emotions with EFT: Tap into Your Hidden Potential with the Emotional Freedom Techniques
by Phillip and Jane Mountrose
A comprehensive self-help book on the EFT and GTT techniques, including chapters on insomnia, pain, addictive habits, improving performance, weight loss, and eliminating stress. "The medicine of the future," says best-selling author Rudolph Ballentine, MD.

Getting Thru to Kids: The Five Steps to Problem Solving with Children Ages 6 to 18 by Phillip Mountrose
Learn five steps to problem-solving with children, improving trust, honesty, school attitude, and friendships. Jack Canfield, co-author of *Chicken Soup for the Soul* series, says, "This wonderful book offers a simple and effective method to create peace and harmony in the home and high self-esteem in your children."

Tips and Tools for Getting Thru Kids: 25 Great Ways to Communicate with Children and Teenagers by Phillip Mountrose
25 dynamic tools that teach parents and educators about themselves as well as their children. A Parents' Choice Winner.

The Holistic Approach to Eating: Lose Extra Weight and Keep It Off for Life by Jane Mountrose
This 82-page booklet provides the keys to losing and maintaining your weight for life. It tells why traditional diets fail

and what really works, so you can make real progress and feel good about yourself.

Ordering information for the above materials is provided at the end of this book.

RECOMMENDED BOOKS

Bradshaw, John. *Homecoming: Reclaiming and Championing Your Inner Child*. New York: Bantam, 1990. A wealth of practical techniques, case histories, and questionnaires from the author's inner child workshops.

Brennan, Barbara Ann. *Hands of Light*. New York: Bantam, 1988. An in-depth study of the human energy field for people who seek happiness, health, and their full potential.

Brennan, Barbara Ann. *Light Emerging*. New York: Bantam, 1993. An exploration of how we can understand and work with our most fundamental healing power: the light that emerges from the very center of our humanity.

Carlson, Richard and Shield, Benjamin, editors. *Handbook for the Soul*. Boston: Little, Brown and Company, 1995. An anthology of writings by some of today's most renowned spiritual teachers that provides new ways to understand and nurture your spiritual side.

Carpenter, Carl. *The Far Side of Hypno-Kinesiology*. Spiral-bound instruction manual, which includes remote clearing, possession therapy, past life research and more. For ordering, contact the author at 603-224-4996.

Carpenter, Carl. *Hypno-Kinesiology for Professionals*. Spiral-bound manual using muscle testing and anchors or ideo motor responses and visualization to locate and release "source traumas" that cause emotional problems. For ordering, contact the author at 603-224-4996.

Diamond, John. *Life Energy*. New York: Paragon House, 1990. A clear presentation of ways to use muscle testing and the meridians to unlock the hidden power of your emotions.

Dossey, Larry. *Recovering the Soul*. New York: Bantam, 1989. A penetrating exploration of the nexus of mysticism and healing, religion and physics that helps us to understand our deepest and most elemental selves.

Lama, Dalai and Cutler, Howard C. *The Art of Happiness*. New York: Riverhead Books, 1998. An inspiring presentation of the importance of happiness as the very purpose of life.

Pearson, Carol S. *The Hero Within*. New York: HarperCollins, 1986. An exploration of literature, anthropology, and psychology that insightfully defines the six heroic archetypes that exist in all of us.

Pearsall, Paul. *The Heart's Code: Tapping the Wisdom and Power of Our Heart Energy*. New York: Broadway Books, 1998. New findings about cellular memories and their role in the mind/body/spirit connection.

Peck, M. Scott. *A World Waiting to be Born*. New York: Bantam, 1993. A guide to a richer understanding of our lives within our families, our workplaces, and our communities.

Richo, David. *Unexpected Miracles, The Gift of Synchronicity and How to Open It*. New York: Crossroad Publishing, 1998. An exploration of how synchronicity works in daily life.

Shepard, Stephen Paul. *Healing Energies*. Provo, Utah: Woodland Health Books, 1983. A system of preventing disease by muscle testing and studying the blueprint of the body.

Stone, Hal and Winkelman, Sidra. *Embracing Our Selves*. San Raphael, California: New World Library, 1989. A guide to the method known as Voice Dialogue, which introduces you to the different selves that live within you.

WEB SITES

The Getting Thru Web Site: This is our site, which has information on Spiritual Kinesiology, EFT, and all the books in the Getting Thru series. You will also find articles and information on other healing techniques, spiritual growth, audio tapes, video tapes, personal consultations, seminars, and two free monthly newsletters.
URL: http://www.gettingthru.org

The Hypno-Kinesiology Web Site: Carl Carpenter, the originator of Hypno-Kinesiology, has developed this site, which contains a description of his methods, kinesiology worksheets, and resources for users of these techniques.
URL: http://www.hypno-kinesiology.com

Glossary

Activation: In relation to any healing process, activation is the final step in the healing process, initiating a greater awareness of oneself. There are seven major activations on the spiritual journey. There are also a number of minor activations that correspond with each of the individual lessons one learns along the way.

Anchoring: An NLP technique that imprints a desired state of mind through the use of one of the five senses, such as sound, sight, or sensation. Spiritual Kinesiology uses a kinesthetic (touch) anchoring.

Apex Problem: An EFT term referring to a form of denial that some people experience in relation to subtle energy techniques. Their limited belief systems do not include the possibility that these techniques could produce rapid and profound change. When the changes occur, these people block out their memories of the former problem.

Archetypes: Images and patterns of behavior that apply to everyone in a particular culture or, in some cases, to the entire human species. The term commonly applies to symbolic images and personality types.

Aura: The energy field.

Chakra: An energy center that extends from the body through all seven levels of the aura or energy field. These centers collect higher frequencies of energy, and step them down through the levels to nourish the aura and the body. There are seven major chakras, along with hundreds of minor chakras all around the body.

Clearing: This involves making efforts to understand a problem so that we can move forward. Energetically, this clearing releases blockages from the energy field, preparing us to embrace more light and soul awareness.

Co-Creation: The ultimate goal of the spiritual journey, which involves living one's divine purpose in each moment and, in so doing, participating consciously in the unfolding of the divine plan for humanity.

Divine Plan: The plan for the evolution of humanity, which is being orchestrated by beings of lights in the higher dimensions, including our guides, the ascended masters and the angels. In our spiritual development, each of us is playing a part in this divine plan.

EFT: Emotional Freedom Techniques. A series of meridian-based healing processes developed by Gary Craig and Adrienne Fowlie, based on the discoveries of Dr. Roger Callahan.

Ego: Generally refers to the wounded ego or false personality, which is the sum of the parts of oneself that have become disconnected from the light and wisdom of the soul by programming and difficult experiences. In this fragmented state, the ego is generally lost in fear and limitation. Its rightful role is as a mediator between the higher dimensional awareness of the soul and the practical requirements of our third dimensional reality. As the fragmented parts of the ego are healed, it returns to this position and the soul moves to the forefront. This healthy ego may also be called the true personality.

Energy Center: Chakra.

Energy Field: The seven layers or levels of energy that surround and interpenetrate the physical body. These layers contain different frequencies of energy that gradually step down in vibration from the higher dimensions where the oversoul exists to the physical body. They define our entire reality.

Energy Toxins: A term that refers to energies and substances that irritate the energy system. Energy toxins include substances that are ingested or in contact with the body, along with negative energies in the environment.

Finger Rolling Technique: A method used in SK either to calm a highly agitated person or to relieve residual blockages after an initial balancing. It involves lightly rolling your fingertips along a person's shoulder and arm.

Getting Thru Techniques: A group of processes developed by Phillip and Jane Mountrose that help individuals bring greater awareness to what is happening in their unconscious minds, to clear any blockages they encounter, and to integrate the changes into their conscious awareness. These processes help individuals to progress in their personal and spiritual growth, with the ultimate goal of achieving joy, love, and freedom in all aspects of life.

GTT: Getting Thru Techniques.

Higher Self: Oversoul.

HK: Hypno-Kinesiology.

Holistic: Related to or concerned with integrated whole or complete systems rather than with analyzing or treating separate parts. In relation to healing, this term commonly refers to dealing with the body, emotions, mind, and spirit as parts of an integrated whole.

Holistic Hypnotherapy: A state-of-the-art approach to hypnotherapy that includes the body, emotions, mind, and spirit. It taps into the vast resources each person has in the unconscious mind that can lead to an expanded sense of fulfillment and wholeness.

Hypno-Kinesiology: A group of techniques developed by hypnotherapist Carl Carpenter that include the use kinesiology (muscle testing) as a diagnostic tool and two methods drawn from hypnotherapy, reframing and anchoring, to deal with issues and imbalances.

Integrating: In the healing process, a period of restructuring that follows clearing. With the clearing, a blockage is released and one's energetic makeup shifts. This shift is followed by a period of integration, which may take from a few minutes to a period of months or years to incorporate the changes into one's conscious awareness.

Kinesiology: The use of muscle testing to access information from the unconscious mind and the body's innate intelligence. It works by testing how the strength of a muscle is affected by focusing on an external stimulus or a part of the body. Kinesiology may be used to test how the body is affected by different substances, environmental factors, and verbal statements.

Mass Consciousness: Agreed-upon beliefs and rules by the majority of people. Much of this agreement is unconscious.

Multi-Dimensional: Refers to having access to other dimensions that exist beyond those that our five senses perceive. The soul resides in these higher dimensions, which we can access with the right willingness and tools.

Muscle Testing: The practical use of kinesiology. By isolating a specific muscle, you can test its response to access conscious and unconscious information.

Neurolinguistic Programming (NLP): A group of techniques and skills that some call the art and science of excellence. NLP includes communication skills that can help anyone to understand how different people experience life, thereby improving both personal and professional relationships. It also includes techniques that are similar to hypnotherapy, which can help with overcoming difficulties and with achieving excellence in all aspects of one's life.

NLP: Neurolinguistic Programming.

Oversoul: The source of the soul that exists in the higher dimensions, which is one's true source of light and wisdom, also known as the higher self.

R&A: Reframing and Anchoring Technique.

Reframing: An NLP technique that refers to clearing blockages by replacing an unbalanced pattern with a balanced one.

Reframing & Anchoring Technique: The balancing part of Spiritual Kinesiology. Reframing and anchoring includes the use of two techniques drawn from hypnotherapy. To strengthen one's relationship with one's soul, it includes a way to anchor in the soul's wisdom and bring oneself more into alignment with one's divine purpose.

Reiki: A hands-on healing approach that sends life force energy to specific areas of the body and the surrounding energy field. Reiki includes techniques to use for the physical, emotional, mental, and spiritual levels of healing, along with long-distance healing.

SK: Spiritual Kinesiology

Soul: The eternal part of oneself that exists beyond the limitations we experience in our third dimensional reality; also known as the true self.

Spiritual Kinesiology: A group of spiritual healing techniques developed by Phillip Mountrose and Jane Mountrose based on the work of Carl Carpenter. Spiritual Kinesiology includes the use of kinesiology (muscle testing) as a diagnostic tool and two methods drawn from hypnotherapy, reframing and anchoring, to bring issues into balance with the light and wisdom of the soul.

Subpersonality: A fragmented part of an individual that has been separated from the wholeness of the soul through difficult or traumatic experiences; sometimes referred to as a "wounded part" or simply a "part."

True Self: Soul.

Index

About the Authors

Phillip and Jane Mountrose have studied and developed self-development and spiritual growth techniques for over twenty-five years. They operate the Awakenings Institute For Holistic Studies, a non-profit organization located in California.

PHILLIP MOUNTROSE is a Special Education Teacher, Holistic Hypnotherapist, Reiki Master, NLP Practitioner, and Minister of Holistic Healing, with over twenty years of classroom experience. He now teaches self-healing and personal growth classes, and works with people individually to help them achieve their goals. He helps people to identify and release their blockages, so they can experience more joy, love and freedom in their lives. He also draws on his extensive teaching experience to help children and families.

Phillip co-wrote *Getting Thru to Your Emotions with EFT* with Jane. He also has written two books for communicating with children, entitled *Getting Thru To Kids* and *Tips and Tools for Getting Thru to Kids*. He has a master's in Education from the University of Massachusetts and a master's in Fine Arts from UCLA. Through his media interviews, classes, and consultations, he continues to provide innovative ways to help people improve communication and fulfill their potential.

JANE MOUNTROSE is a Holistic Hypnotherapist, Reiki Master, Clairvoyant Counselor, and Minister of Holistic Healing with over twenty years of experience as an architect and artist.

In recent years, Jane has focused her attention on helping people to achieve their full potential and live their divine purposes. Her classes in personal and spiritual growth provide easy-to-use tools derived from Holistic Hypnotherapy, NLP, Reiki, EFT, Spiritual Kinesiology, and clairvoyant reading skills.

Jane co-wrote *Getting Thru to Your Emotions with EFT* with Phillip. Her consultations include clairvoyant reading, EFT, Holistic Hypnotherapy, Spiritual Kinesiology, and energetic healing. This unique combination of techniques helps her clients to connect more profoundly with their souls and reach their full potentials. Jane has also overcome a lifelong weight problem that stayed with her until she was in her forties. She now helps people with a holistic approach to eating that helps them to lose weight and keep it off for life.

CLASSES AND CONSULTATIONS

Phillip and Jane Mountrose teach classes and seminars in EFT, Reiki, Spiritual Kinesiology, the Getting Thru Techniques, and spiritual development. They also offer personal consultations to help people to connect more deeply with their spiritual journeys and their divine purposes.

Many people think that reaching out to others for assistance is a sign of weakness. This is far from the truth. Along with developing a relationship with our true divine selves, we can all benefit from the loving input of others as we progress on the spiritual journey. Phillip and Jane focus on making a life filled with joy, love and freedom a reality for those who come into contact with them.

For more information about scheduling personal consultations, speaking engagements, and seminars contact:

Phillip and Jane Mountrose
P.O. Box 279, Arroyo Grande, CA 93421-0279
E-mail: awake@gettingthru.org Phone Messages: (800) 644-5437

Phillip and Jane also welcome your communication, especially your experiences, insights, challenges, and successes with the interactive tools in this book. You can also visit their Web site at:

www.gettingthru.org.

Order Form

ITEM	QUANTITY	COST
Getting Thru to Your Soul:		
• Book $14.95	_____	_____
• Two Audio Tapes $16.95	_____	_____
Getting Thru to Your Soul Videos:		
• Part 1: SK & the Basic Techniques $24.95	_____	_____
• Part 2: Inner Child & Relationships $24.95	_____	_____
• Part 3: Archetypes & Subpersonalites $24.95	_____	_____
• Parts 1, 2, 3 Videos together $59.95	_____	_____
Getting Thru to Your Emotions:		
• Book $13.95	_____	_____
• Two Audio Tapes $16.95	_____	_____
Getting Thru to Your Emotions Videos:		
• Part 1: The EFT Techniques: Video $24.95	_____	_____
• Part 2: The GTT Techniques: Video $24.95	_____	_____
• Part 1 and Part 2 Videos together $39.95	_____	_____
Tips & Tools for Getting Thru to Kids:		
• Book $ 12.95	_____	_____
• 2-Tape AudioBook $ 16.95	_____	_____
Getting Thru to Kids		
• Book $11.95	_____	_____
• 2-Tape AudioBook $16.95	_____	_____
Holistic Approach to Eating: Booklet $10	_____	_____

SUBTOTAL _____

US Shipping $3.50 first item, $.50 each additional item _____
For shipping out of the U.S., $8 for first item,
$6 each additional item.

California residents please add 7.75% for sales tax _____

AMOUNT ENCLOSED _____

Order Form (con't)

QUANTITY DISCOUNTS are available on bulk purchases of this book for educational training purposes, fund raising, or gift giving. For information contact the publisher.

<u>Free</u> Email Newsletters (check selections):
Getting Thru to Your Soul __   Getting Thru to Those You Love __
E-mail address: _____

Ship to:

Name: _____

Company: _____

Address: _____

City:_____State: _____

Zip: _____Phone:(_____)_____

Payment:

___ Check   ___ Money Order

Credit Card: ___ Visa   ___ Mastercard   ___ Discover

Card Number: _____

Name on Card: _____

Expiration Date: _____/_____

Mail To: Holistic Communications
        P.O. Box 279
        Arroyo Grande, CA 93421-0279

Toll-Free 24 Hour Order Line: (800) 644-5437

For more information, visit our Web site: www.gettingthru.org

Money Back Guarantee!